The Disturbances

The Disturbances

The Untold Story of How Missionaries Saved Lives in a Time of Tribal Genocide

Robert Parham

Baptist Center for Ethics
EthicsDaily.com
Nashville, Tennessee

Baptist Center for Ethics
EthicsDaily.com
P.O. Box 150506
Nashville, Tennessee 37215-0506

© Baptist Center for Ethics 2016
All rights reserved. First printing 2016.
Printed in the United States of America.

The Baptist Center for Ethics is a free-standing network of trained ethicists, ministers and educators, providing resources and services to congregations, clergy and educational institutions. Contact info@ethicsdaily.com for more information.

Cover image: Southern Baptist missionary Bob Parham comforts a Nigerian girl during the Jos airlift in 1966. Photo courtesy: SIM International Archives.

Copyright © 2016 Robert Parham
All rights reserved.

ISBN: 0997892404
ISBN 13: 9780997892406
Library of Congress Control Number: 2016912544
Baptist Center for Ethics, Nashville, TN

Table of Contents

Acknowledgments · vii
Preface · ix
Introduction · xv

Chapter 1   Arrival of Missionaries, Birth of a Nation · · · · · · · · · · · · · · 1
Chapter 2   Trip to Zaria · 11
Chapter 3   Some Igbos Flee from the North, Others Decide to Stay · · · · 18
Chapter 4   Uncertainties and Tensions Escalate · · · · · · · · · · · · · · · · 27
Chapter 5   Tensions Crest · 32
Chapter 6   It Has Started · 38
Chapter 7   Hiding the Igbos · 45
Chapter 8   Second Night, Second Day in Jos · · · · · · · · · · · · · · · · · · · 54
Chapter 9   Violence Winds Down · 61
Chapter 10 Police Compound Becomes A Sanctuary for Fleeing Igbos · · 66
Chapter 11 Sunday at the Police Compound · 74
Chapter 12 Mission to the Military Supreme Commander · · · · · · · · · · · 97
Chapter 13 Jos Evacuation · 100
Chapter 14 Outside Jos: More Atrocities, More Rescues · · · · · · · · · · · · 104
Chapter 15 Smuggling Igbos Across Jos to the Airport · · · · · · · · · · · · · 114
Chapter 16 Rescue of Hycenth Adibenma · 118
Chapter 17 Jos Notebook: What Is Genocide? · · · · · · · · · · · · · · · · · · · 120
Chapter 18 Conflict Was Tribal, Not Religious · · · · · · · · · · · · · · · · · · · 125
Chapter 19 It Was Planned, But Who Planned It? · · · · · · · · · · · · · · · · 132
Chapter 20 Shock and Silence Set In · 138
Chapter 21 Rescue and Redemption · 146
Chapter 22 Role of Missionaries in a Time of Genocide · · · · · · · · · · · · 151

           Timeline of Events · 157
           Glossary of Terms · 159

Acknowledgments

The staff of Baptist Center for Ethics thanks the board of directors for its support and encouragement. They saw the value of the project from historical and contemporary vantage points. They gave us the freedom to pursue this project—the documentary and the book.

A special word of acknowledgement and gratitude goes to the Eula Mae and John Baugh Foundation, which underwrote the lion's share of expenses. Without the Baugh Foundation's support, the quality and depth of content of this project would not have been possible. We are also thankful to the many individual financial contributors and foundations who helped fund this effort.

A number of missionaries and missionary children (now middle-aged adults) trusted us with their memories, correspondence, diaries, photographs and film footage. While we did video interviews with some 25 missionaries and missionary children, we communicated with a much larger number. We found open hearts and an eagerness to share their experiences. Their collaboration ensured that we got the story right.

Neither the book nor the documentary would have been possible without the diligent work of Cliff Vaughn. He probed deeply into archival material, catalogued video interviews, meticulously checked facts, stitched together a clear narrative and managed the documentary's production. The book followed most of the film script that he wrote.

Zach Dawes read and re-read chapters, improving the quality of the story telling. Michael Leathers proofread the manuscript, making it as error free as humanly possible. Jake Moore and Alayna Hudson, our summer interns, added their insight to the manuscript.

"The Disturbances," the book, goes into much more depth than is possible in the documentary. More accounts are recorded, richer historical details are added, and greater contextual color is provided.

We hope our book and documentary will bring to light one of the most compelling missionary contributions in the 20th century.

All royalties from the sale of this book go to the Baptist Center for Ethics, a 501(c)(3) organization. Proceeds will enable the Baptist Center for Ethics, better known through its website as EthicsDaily.com, to continue its public witness and work for the advancement of the common good.

Robert Parham

Preface

Three fragmentary childhood memories, cryptic family correspondence and a handful of photographs gave birth to two years of meticulous research into what happened in Nigeria in 1966.

The first memory was a man rushing into my seventh-grade classroom at an interdenominational mission school in Jos. The second was seeing villagers carrying on their heads electrical items—record players and fans—into a village without electricity. The third was hearing, at a police station on a Sunday afternoon, an unexpected biblical admonition.

The cryptic family correspondence included a letter from a ranking member of the Foreign Mission Board of the Southern Baptist Convention to my mother's parents. He assured them that there was "no cause for alarm." He simply referred to what was going on in Nigeria as "the disturbances."

In a letter to this executive a week later, my father wrote about "mass killings of Ibos by northerners." He spoke of counting dead bodies in the town. He said that they had heard of hundreds of bodies in the morgue. He added, "All that has happened during those few days cannot be given in this letter."

The handful of black-and-white photographs included frames of my father directing activities at the Jos airport. One showed him speaking to a crying Nigerian woman on a stretcher.

My family never discussed what happened during those days in Jos. My father never shared what he saw when he drove through our town or what he did during an evacuation airlift. Never. Not even years later, long after I was an adult.

For years, I've wanted to know the full story. I knew that something awful had happened. I knew that members of one tribe had formed gangs that generally hunted and butchered members of another tribe. That was about all I really knew.

I raised the question with my colleague, Cliff Vaughn, about whether we could find sufficient material to do a documentary on this story. We had a successful record of producing documentaries on a variety of issues. These documentaries had aired on TV and been widely viewed in churches.

I wondered if we—EthicsDaily.com—would be able to stitch something together. What was the full story surrounding these three items? Were there other accounts? Had any books been written on what had happened in Jos? What about articles? Did the few living Nigerian missionaries have their own experiences? Could they remember them? Would they share them on camera? Did other photographs exist? What about correspondence similar to my family's letters?

We soon discovered that few publicly available books had been written on the subject—and those were about the politics of the events. None developed the story of what missionaries had witnessed and done. With few exceptions, missionaries hadn't written about it. They didn't talk about it at their reunions. Their children didn't discuss it. As a result, their story had slipped into the ether.

We wondered why—why was there so much silence about what had happened?

Cliff and I dug into the story. We searched for books and articles. We made cold calls. We spoke with missionaries. We posted messages on Facebook and followed leads. I called classmates with whom I had not spoken in decades. The more we pressed, the more we found. The more we found, the more we knew this untold story demanded telling.

For the first time in 50 years, a host of missionaries and missionary children are speaking publicly—eagerly.

A few eyewitnesses still think it imprudent to speak openly about what happened in 1966. They suggest that it is too dangerous for missionaries and Nigerians, especially given the terrorism of Boko Haram. One missionary pilot declined to speak on the record, although he shared valuable details. A missionary child, now an adult, wondered why we would now want to record the accounts of what happened.

The vast majority of eyewitnesses, however, weighed the balance. They decided to embrace the wisdom found in Ecclesiastes: "For everything there is a season … a time to keep silence, and a time to speak."

These missionary and missionary children eyewitnesses showed courage in 1966 and again by speaking of encounters long buried. Some showed emotion in recalling the events. All readily shared with us items that had been stored away for years—correspondence, diaries, memos, photographs and film footage. One even gave us a notebook in shorthand chronicling a critical meeting. They recommended others to call. Nigerians, too, shared what they experienced—and encouraged the project. Many sat through long video interviews.

We obtained over 2,500 photographs, rolls of 8mm and 16mm film footage, a mountain of documents. We had scores of conversations. We conducted 25 video interviews.

Cliff and I have wondered if today's church has the courage to hear their gritty stories, even to consider that some missionaries struggled to reconcile how brother could have killed brother given the longstanding endeavor of Christian missionaries to promote brotherhood among diverse tribal or ethnic groups.

We hope the Christian community will come to a deeper understanding of missionaries, who are, as outsiders, vulnerable to national events and disposed to feel responsible for the most vulnerable around them. Nothing could have prepared these men and women for what they encountered and how they reacted. Yet they did so wisely and at great risk because it was the right thing to do.

We also hope the Christian community will arrive at a more informed understanding of genocide. Genocide is rooted in prejudice, deliberately planned and executed, and designed to eliminate a group of people based on their ethnicity, race or religion. It is not spontaneous or random. It's organized, plotted, brutal.

It happens over and over again. After each genocidal episode, governmental and international leaders pledge "never again." But the pledge is seldom kept. And few leaders of genocide are ever prosecuted. Surely, it is time for the Christian community to determine that it must serve as "watchmen on the gate."

The title for our documentary and this accompanying book is "The Disturbances." The choice of the title and the strange squiggly line will become clear later on.

For now, read this untold story. Be warned, it contains graphic details. Yet it's an incredible story about ruin and redemption, rumor and reaction, blood and boldness, denial and dedication, guilt and goodness.

Introduction

This is a true story kept quiet by missionaries, unknown to church members, unmentioned in the list of genocides over the past 50 years.

Yet it deserves a place in the histories of human atrocities and the chronicles of Christian history. We need to remember both the capacity for planned and executed human evil, as well as the potential for calculated and courageous human goodness.

For the sake of this story, we begin six years after Nigeria was granted independence from Great Britain in 1960. One could rightly critique European colonialism and the 1884 Berlin conference that haphazardly carved up sub-Saharan Africa. They ignored tribal boundaries. They overlooked historical and religious relationships. They disregarded linguistic regions. That history is well documented. That field has been abundantly plowed. Additionally, the steady negative drumbeat about the missionary enterprise is well known. We have no intention to join the scrum over colonialism and missions.

Less well known is what happened when Nigerian military officers toppled in January 1966 the elected leadership of "Africa's giant." Tribal tensions immediately re-emerged. Most of the coup d'etat military officers were members of the Igbo tribe. Those assassinated included ranking members of the Hausa tribe.

Max Siollun, in his book, *Oil, Politics and Violence*, puts it this way: "The overwhelming majority of the January plotters were Igbo, most of their victims were non-Igbo."

Igbo civilians were then killed in late May in northern Nigeria, where Hausas predominantly lived, reportedly out of revenge and displeasure over a new government decree. The decree limited regional power, something Northerners opposed. A second coup occurred in July. It replaced the country's supreme commander, who was an Igbo, with a member of a northern tribe. In September, widespread genocide was launched. An estimated 30,000 Igbos would be massacred over the course of a few days in 1966. Of course, no one knows the exact count.

Hundreds of thousands of Igbos would flee to the Eastern Region of Nigeria, their traditional homeland, even though many had been born and raised in the Northern Region, the Hausa homeland.

The atrocities triggered the Eastern Region to withdraw from the federal government of Nigeria. A brutal three-year civil war was fought, known as the Biafran War. An estimated 1.5 million Easterners would die, mostly from starvation.

Southern Baptist missionary Bryant Durham remained in Biafra throughout the war as a leader of the Christian humanitarian relief effort. He would write in his dissertation at the University of Georgia a few years later that 3,000 to 4,000 civilian deaths occurred every day between August and October 1968. By November 1969, the daily death toll had dropped to 1,000 to 2,000. The numbers are staggering.

Nigerian historian Godfrey Uzoigwe, an Igbo with a doctor of philosophy degree from Oxford University, has written that the Igbo genocide "dwarfed the Congolese killings of the early 1960s, the Tutsi genocide of the early 1990s and the more recent Darfur genocide, in its hatred, planning, intensity, ferocity, barbarity and the number of people killed or affected. But genocide scholars have totally ignored it."

Sadly, the church doesn't know what missionaries did to save lives during these brutal days in 1966. Aside from private correspondence, minutes, fragmentary references in newspaper articles, and brief notes in a few books, their story is unrecorded.

"The Disturbances" is their story.

Speaking at a Jewish Heritage Week in April 1985, President Ronald Reagan presented the Congressional Gold Medal to Elie Wiesel. He noted that the American people had pledged after the Holocaust: "Never again."

"To say 'never again,' however, is not enough," said Reagan. "…[O]ur pledge was more than 'Never again.' It was also, 'Never forget.'"

Yet Reagan stood by as Guatemala's president committed genocide against his own indigenous people.

President George H. W. Bush remained inactive as Serbia sought to ethnically cleanse Bosnia.

President Bill Clinton said at the Holocaust Memorial Museum that the United States must never permit such an event again. Yet he stood by while hundreds of thousands of Tutsis were slaughtered in Rwanda.

President George W. Bush declared in 2004 at the Holocaust Memorial Museum about Darfur: "It is evil we are now seeing in Sudan – and we're not going to back down."

xvii

Many argue that the targeting of Christians in the Middle East, Syria in particular, by ISIS is genocide. Yet President Barack Obama has skirted the word.

"Never again" rings hollow. Genocide continues. It does so perhaps because perpetrators have learned that Western governments and the international community are reluctant to intervene. Perpetrators may believe that they will go unpunished.

In a world of genocide, the global church's task is both to be a watchman on the gate to warn of genocide and to press governments and international bodies to intervene.

While our story is set in the midst of the Nigerian genocide, it is not primarily about genocide, the politics of tribal targeting, or even the root causes.

No, our work is really about missionaries and their children—what they witnessed and did to save lives. We chronicle stories of how missionaries hid Igbos at great personal risk from roving Hausa gangs with machetes, how they transported Igbos across dangerous ground to safety. We recall how missionary children—high school students—tended to the wounds of butchered victims and sang hymns to those who died in their arms. We explore rescue stories: with endings still unresolved, others with tearful remains. We tell stories of redemption.

"The Disturbances" is both horrifying and inspiring.

Chapter 1

Arrival of Missionaries, Birth of a Nation

The first Christian missionaries to Nigeria were Portuguese monks, arriving in the territory that became Nigeria in the 15th century.

In 1842, Anglican clergyman Henry Townsend, with the Church Missionary Society, began sowing the seeds of Christianity in West Africa. He and a Yoruba ex-slave, Samuel Ajayi Crowther, settled in Abeokuta, a city in the Yoruba tribal homeland, in Nigeria's southwest.

Thomas Jefferson Bowen, from the State of Georgia, soon followed. He arrived in Nigeria in 1850 as a Southern Baptist missionary, only five years after the formation of the Southern Baptist Convention. He, too, put down roots in the homeland of the Yoruba tribe. He learned the Yoruba language and even published a Yoruba grammar. He baptized his first convert in 1854.

The harsh conditions in Nigeria—tribal conflict, the slave trade, and health challenges—made mission work hard. From Bowen's arrival until 1890, few missionaries were appointed to what was known as the "white man's graveyard."

After the turn of the century, things began to change in terms of baptisms and church growth, mostly among the Yorubas, and rapid growth began in the mid-20th century. By 1955, Southern Baptists had almost 200 missionaries in Nigeria engaged in elementary and high school education, medical missions, evangelism, and the training of pastors.

Nigerian Baptists paid homage to Bowen when they named the largest Baptist university in Africa after him.

Although Catholicism came to Nigeria in the 15th century, it had "virtually disappeared by the 17th century." Catholic priests came first to the Yoruba city of Lagos in 1865 and then to Benin in 1870, where the Edo or Bini tribe predominated. They established work in Onitsha, in the Igbo tribal area, in 1885.

"Catholic schools grew increasingly popular; while Protestant mission schools taught in local languages, Catholic schools promoted English, which was regarded as a means of advancement in colonial society by the Igbo," according to Harvard Divinity School's "Catholicism in Nigeria."

The article reported that "over half of the Catholic missions in Nigeria were located in the eastern region," which became the Igbo homeland in the later 1960s.

Missionary Charles Fuller wrote that the Sudan Interior Mission (also known as Soudan Interior Mission) had multiple founders toward the end of the 18th century. The SIM's first representatives to Nigeria arrived in December 1893. Facing health challenges and death, the first two SIM efforts failed. However, the first successful mission station was opened in 1902 among the Nupe tribe.

The Christian Reformed Church missionaries arrived in Nigeria in 1905, thanks to the collaboration with the Sudan United Mission, which had entered the country a year earlier. Two missionaries planted their work in Wukari. One learned the Hausa language; the other the Jukun language. They did evangelistic outreach, established an orphanage, started educational efforts, and provided health care.

The first Lutheran missionaries to Nigeria were Danish, arriving in 1913. They, too, worked with the Sudan United Mission.

The earliest Church of the Brethren missionaries came to Nigeria in 1922. They settled in Garkida, a northeastern village where the tribal language was Bura. Like Southern Baptists and Christian Reformed, they engaged in education and medical work.

Everett and Dorothy Phillips joined these different denominational missions in 1936. They were with the Assemblies of God, although the Pentecostal movement had begun in Nigeria in 1920.

Phillips recorded an experience with a Nigerian who said that his grandfather had met a prophet who told him to put away idols and expect the arrival of a man with a book that would show a better way. The Nigerian asked Phillips, "Are you the man with the book?" Phillips answered, "Yes." Raising his Bible, he said, "This is the book."

Christianity flourished in southern Nigeria among the Yoruba tribe, which lived in the West, and the Igbo tribe, which lived in the East. It also spread to the North, where the Hausa and Fulani tribes dominated.

Nigeria had 250 tribes within its national boundaries. Each was unique in its traditions, practices, environmental influences, and opportunities.

The former chancellor of Bowen University, Timothy Olagbemiro, described the tribal differences. "The Hausas and Fulanis are different…The Fulani were cattle-raisers…the Yoruba are mainly businessmen…The Igbos…

were into education…The Hausas are mainly sellers…People who hire bicycles out." Hausas were also tailors.

"Many Igbos were doctors and nurses…The Hausas…were not as forward in terms of education as others…The people who actually did farming in the area of Jos are the Berums…the Berums are the indigents of Jos," he said.

Noting Nigeria's large population, one interviewee, an Assemblies of God missionary, Jerry Falley, said, "In a general sense, the Nigerians—by and large compared with other African countries—are aggressive. The Igbos are super aggressive. But the other groups, too, the Yoruba, the Hausa. Those are aggressive groups. I think the aggressiveness, the desire for action, on the part of the Nigerian is a defining characteristic."

"With the Igbos, education was a defining characteristic. They put a lot of value on it. They were very successful…The Hausas were not necessarily less intelligent, but they had less opportunity. The school system in the East was much more advanced…They were really thirsty for education. The Hausa, they tended to be more rural," added Falley. He noted that the Catholic and Anglican churches were very strong in the East, while the North was predominantly Muslim.

"The Igbos were business oriented. But because of the education, they had opportunity to serve in civil service and they sort of dominated the civil service," said Falley. "The British had not prepared the Hausa for that responsibility."

Another interviewee, Jo Ann Parham, a Baptist missionary, agreed with Falley's observation about education and civil service jobs. She said, "I think the Igbos were more eager for education and more willing to sacrifice for it." It was education that opened up work for the civil service.

When Lutheran missionary Beverly Knuth was interviewed, she said the Igbos "were more well educated…in a much more populated area in the East…Schools made more sense because there were lots of people in a smaller area…They had a better start in life. Same thing is true for the Yoruba…In the North, people are so spread out."

The people of the North were "more nomadic. Fulani people wander with their herds. They don't settle in any one place. Their children don't get an education," she said.

Knuth contended that the Igbos were not more intelligent than the Hausas or other tribes. But the Igbos' success had to do with "circumstance."

She didn't see the Hausa and Fulani as anti-education. "They just didn't have the opportunity. It wasn't there."

Interviewees—missionaries and others—emphasized the role that Christian and British education played in giving Igbos opportunities in civil service jobs—such as running the post offices, the water, electrical and telephone systems, and the airports. Educational opportunities would contribute to later conflict.

By the mid-20th century, Christian missionaries had worked in Nigeria for more than a century. They established a presence alongside Islam and paganism—paganism or traditional religions were widespread across Nigeria. The missionaries built churches, started hospitals, orphanages and leprosy settlements, established schools, trained pastors, translated the Bible into different tribal languages, did evangelistic programs. They sought to improve agricultural production to improve the nutrition of Nigerians.

They also started in Jos an interdenominational mission boarding school for missionary children that would provide education from the 1st grade through the 12th grade.

Started in 1942 with 12 students by the Church of the Brethren, Hillcrest School students went without textbooks the first year. During World War II, submarines sank boats with the first two shipments of books.

By 1966, the Assemblies of God, Christian Reformed Church, Church of the Brethren, Lutheran Church-Missouri Synod, American Lutheran Mission, Southern Baptist Convention, U.M.S. (United Methodist), and Sudan United Mission were sponsoring the school.

The student body included day students, as well as non-Christian students—Muslims and Hindus, whose parents were local merchants. Younger students lived on campus. Older students—generally high school students—lived in hostels off campus, scattering across the city.

Some 15 miles from Hillcrest was another mission boarding school, Kent Academy, sponsored by the Sudan Interior Mission (today known as Serving In Mission). It was located in the remote village of Miango.

As the missionary enterprise took form, so did the territory that would become Nigeria. Nigeria was a nation created by the European colonial powers.

In 1884, European nations met in Berlin with the American government in attendance. The gathering carved up Africa with little appreciation for tribes, languages, historical relationships, and religions. Germany controlled Tanganyika (now Tanzania). Italy governed most of modern-day Somalia and Eritrea. Britain had the West African "Gold Coast," including Nigeria, plus Kenya, Uganda, and Rhodesia (Zimbabwe). France had the "Ivory Coast" and most of Sahel (sub-Saharan Africa). The Belgians got the Congo—and later Rwanda from Germany. The Portuguese lorded over Mozambique and Angola. Europe extracted the wealth of Africa and installed colonial governance.

The conference itself sowed the seeds of widespread conflict.

The Disturbances

In northern Nigeria, the Hausa are the dominant group and Islam is the dominant religion. Other large Northern tribes are the Fulani and Kanuri.

A popular narrative is that the British favored the feudal system of Islam in northern Nigeria, discouraging Western missionaries from establishing mission stations there. British official Frederick Lugard did restrict missionaries in the Kano area. Both British and Muslim authorities sought to segregate outsiders to sections at the edge of towns called "sabon gari."

As is often the case, popular narratives are not always the most accurate narrative, especially in a complex world.

"Northern Nigeria was not inhospitable to Christianity…Yet Christianity…did not have followers until the colonial era, when European and American missionaries established schools, hospitals and churches," observed Shoban Shankar in *Who Shall Enter Paradise?*

After the Second World War, colonies began to push for independence. Nigeria gained its independence from Britain in October 1960.

As a child living in the northern city of Kaduna with my missionary parents, I remember that year. Princess Alexandra rode by our missionary home, waving to the crowds lining the road. An influx of Nigerians from rural parts of the North surged into the city.

During the celebration, a trader came to our home with a young muzzled and blind hyena for sale. Despite my pleading, my father refused to buy the hyena for me as a pet. It was one of my first memories of disappointment with my parents. Nonetheless, I relished the enthusiastic celebration—horsemen in turbans, a marching military band, indigenous drummers, and colorful wardrobes.

Known as the "African giant," Nigeria had some 250 distinct tribes with almost 400 different languages. It was managed initially by Britain's Royal Niger

Company, which derived its name from the Niger River, the largest of two primary rivers that intersected the country. The Niger stretches across much of West Africa. The other river, the Benue, reaches toward Central Africa.

The name for Nigeria came from the wife of the first British governor-general, Sir Frederick Lugard.

One of the major fault lines in Nigeria was the division between the southern part of the country, which was seen as mostly Christian, and the northern part, which was mostly Islamic, with traditional African religions spread across the land.

The South thrived with colonial and missionary education. The North was much slower to embrace Western education. The North, however, had had written records in the city of Kano dating back to 900 A.D.

Uniting such a diverse nation demanded a unifying language. English became the national language. It also required a transformative national anthem. That anthem included the promise: "Though tribe and tongue may differ, in brotherhood we stand."

Nigerian leaders recognized the potential tribal conflict.

Missionaries, too, played a role in advancing unity. The Jos Baptist High School had a motto drawn from Psalm 133:1—"Behold, how good and how pleasant it is for brethren to dwell together in unity!"

Unity, however, demanded more than a common language, a promising anthem, and missionary efforts across all tribal groups and regions.

After independence, regional strife boiled over. A census triggered controversy. Tribal accusations sharpened. Then in January 1966, a military coup overthrew the democratically elected government.

The Disturbances

Cornell Goerner, secretary for Africa, Europe and the Near East for the Foreign Mission Board of the Southern Baptist Convention, circled January 15 on his calendar with a note: "Nigerian coup."

Baptist medical missionary Ruth Berrey wrote him on January 16: "The coup d'etat has provided us with cloak and dagger games the last few days. We were advised to be ready to flee so everybody packed a bag. Food and water was put in cars."

She added, "We thought the North was quiet so we were very much surprised to hear that the Sardauna, his wife, his general and wife were killed. There had been so much disturbance in the west we really weren't surprised to hear the Akintola was dead. A lot of bad things were done by him or in his name but he was always friendly and kind to us."

The Sardauna was Ahmadu Bello, the premier of Northern Nigeria who carried the title Sardauna of Sokoto. He was a Northerner and Muslim.

Samuel Ladoke Akintola was a member of the Yoruba tribe who was born in Ogbomosho, a Western city. He was educated in Baptist schools and was known as a founding father of Nigeria.

Another Northerner assassinated was Abubakar Tafawa Balewa, who was the prime minister of Nigeria.

A number of Northerners (Hausas) and Westerners (Yorubas) were assassinated. Most of the coup leaders were from the Eastern Region—and Igbos.

In a form letter, Goerner wrote on January 17, "There has been unrest and a certain amount of lawlessness up until the time of this coup. Now that the army has taken over it is probable that order has been completely restored."

In another form letter dated January 20, he wrote that he had received a cablegram from Carl Whirley, convention secretary for the Northern Region of Nigeria: "All missionaries in Kaduna and Northern Region safe working normally anticipate no trouble please inform families."

Goerner concluded: "Apparently the entire country is now peaceful, the new government has things under control."

Such was not the case, however. Tribal animosity deepened. Unrest became the order of the day.

Chapter 2

Trip to Zaria

Three missionaries had missed their late May flight from Jos to the international airport in Kano for their return trip to the United States. Married only a year, Judy and Joel Hollingshead were short-term medical missionaries with the Church of the Brethren, who had finished a 10-week assignment in Garkida. The other was Carol Leigh Humphries, a Southern Baptist, who headed up work with the Woman's Missionary Union in Northern Nigeria.

Southern Baptist missionary Bob Parham decided to drive them on a Sunday to Kano to catch their flight. He asked Buzz Bowers, a Church of the Brethren missionary, to accompany him. They left in a blue 404 Peugeot station wagon, which had three rows of seats.

Harold "Buzz" Bowers was in the United States Air Force stationed in North Africa when he met his future wife, Shirley Bishop, who was in the Corps of Engineers. They had met in Casablanca while singing Christmas carols in 1953. Upon their return to the United States, they wed and wove their way through military service and a Brethren college. A professor introduced him to the idea of teaching in Nigeria.

The Bowers arrived in Nigeria in January 1965 with the assignment of teaching English in the Waka teacher-training college. The next year, they became temporary house parents at Boulder Hill Hostel in Jos.

"I rode shotgun on that trip," said Bowers, noting that they were driving during the dusty time of the year.

Nigeria had two seasons: dry season and rainy season. During the dry season, dust, known as Harmattan, blew southward from the Sahara Desert. When it arrived, it caked everything. Given the narrow, often dirty roads, car windows had to be rolled up when passing other vehicles in an effort to reduce clouds kicked up as dust. Even with windows closed, the dust was inescapable.

Heading north from Jos meant even more dust. Jos was a city in the "middle belt" that straddled the North and South with both a significant Christian and Muslim population, with members of many different tribes—and a large missionary presence. Jos was on a plateau known for its cooler weather.

Parham, Bowers and their passengers were going deeper into the territory of the Hausa tribe, which dominated Northern Nigeria.

As they approached the city of Zaria, they began to see disturbing sights.

"We saw smoke. We saw fires and cars overturned. We realized we were driving into a riot…very shocking," said Bowers. "We saw injured people," who they recognized as Igbos.

"I was told not to use my camera too prominently. It might attract attention to us…taking pictures of this terrible specter we were seeing," said Bowers.

Given the unexpected turmoil and the uncertainty of what was taking place, they determined to seek safety at the Baptist mission compound in Zaria.

Jo Ann Parham remembered her husband's trip. "The car in front of them was turned over and the people were killed. They came to the car that Bob and the others were in and started shaking it…Somehow Bob persuaded them not to turn their car over."

When they finally managed to get to the Baptist compound, they found that one of the missionaries was out preaching and probably unaware of what was happening.

That missionary, Art Compere, was new to Nigeria, having arrived with his family in 1965. He was in Zaria at the language school learning Hausa.

Writing a few days later about what happened in May, Compere told his parents, "I packed up my Bible, song book, sermon notes, a tire pump and an adjustable wrench in a leather bag, slung it over the handle bar of the bike and started for the village of Kwangila where I had been attending and was to preach that morning."

No sooner had the dismissal prayer occurred at the Hausa church than "Bob Parham, a missionary from Jos, stuck his head in the door and asked to talk to me. He said there was a riot in town, that Doris and the children were safe at home, but that I should come with him…He explained something in Hausa to the pastor. We then left in a hurry."

"He said the mob was not anti-white, but to be safe we should stay at home until it subsided," wrote Compere.

He explained that the reason Parham wanted to drive him to safety was that "on my bike I would have no protection against thrown rocks, bottles, etc."

Compere shared with his parents that another missionary couple, the Palmers, had been at a Yoruba church that day. They said that when the mob passed the church, it created such fear that they—the Yorubas—"ran over church pews and each other trying to hide in the choir loft and other places in the church."

When the Palmers returned to the Baptist compound, they told of "horrid street fighting, pillaging and looting," wrote Compere.

Closing his letter, Art Compere said that his wife, Doris, saw a sign saying, "One North, one People."

"It might stay confined to the north," he added, "but the Ibos in the East might retaliate by killing a few Hausas in the East."

Jo Ann Parham wrote in her memoirs in 2016 about the Zaria trip. She said, "That day stores were ransacked. Filling stations destroyed. Fires raged in parts of town. Later it was reported that anyone—doctor, nurse, patient, custodian, lab technician or aid inside the local hospital, teacher, student, headmaster or headmistress in any school, shop keeper, clerk, household help, gardener, watchman—who was Igbo had been slaughtered using machetes, clubs, sticks and stones."

As the missionaries sought shelter in the Baptist compound, they heard rumors that similar violence was heading to Jos. Parham and Bowers decided to head home. Missionary James Yarbrough offered to drive the three missionaries to Kano.

On their return trip, Parham stopped cars heading into Zaria to warn them of the riots.

"The first vehicle he stopped had a European and two Nigerians in it," said Jo Ann Parham. "He asked the European to walk aside with him and talk to him about if he could trust the people with him. The man said he felt he could trust one and wasn't sure about the other. So Parham said that with what was going on in Zaria, you might want to turn around and go back. The man replied, 'I'm sorry. I can't. I'm the chief of police there.'"

Bowers, too, recalled Parham stopping vehicles heading into Zaria and warning them of the danger. One vehicle, perhaps the one with the chief of police, had diplomatic plates with the driver being an Igbo.

Upon arrival in Jos, Parham and Bowers discovered that it was peaceful. The riots had not come to Jos. The Zaria rumors were wrong.

The Zaria violence etched an unforgettable and deeply disturbing memory with Baptist Mary Futrell. She was a Baptist laywoman from Kentucky with a Ph.D. in biochemistry. She was on faculty at the city's four-year-old Ahmadu Bello University, a school named after the Hausa premier of Northern Nigeria, who had been assassinated only a few months earlier.

She and her husband, Maurice, were at the university at the invitation of the United States Department of Agriculture. The U.S. government sought to improve agricultural production through farming initiatives and educational programs throughout the developing world.

The agriculture department called Maurice Futrell and offered him an invitation to teach in Nigeria. He went home to discuss the offer with his wife.

She recalled that they decided to pray about the opportunity and to read their Bible together. They opened the Bible to Joshua 1:9—"Be strong and of good courage; be not afraid." Convinced that God had a hand in their decision, they accepted the invitation, arriving in Nigeria in 1964.

Both taught. She was hired to teach nutrition to Nigerian schoolgirls.

When the atrocities erupted in Zaria, she witnessed a shocking event.

"There was one Igbo faculty member in the school of agriculture," she said. On Monday after the Sunday massacres and looting, "I was going to my class. About half way there, this group came up that had their machetes...I don't know if they went to his office or asked him to come outside. But they did cut his head off. And I saw it."

Zaria was not the only city where Igbos were violently killed, their homes looted and businesses burned. Gombe and Sokoto underwent similar atrocities.

Catholic missionaries reported outbreaks of violence against Igbos in Sokoto, in far northwestern Nigeria, closer to Niamey, Niger, than to Kano, and in Gombe, northeast of Jos.

According to a United States Department of State cablegram dated May 30, Father Shea relayed from Sokoto that the Catholic church and residence had been "completely sacked."

"Father Shea estimates at least 1,000 Ibos homeless and now gathered at the police barracks for protection. 180 houses and shops almost all smashed and looted," read the telegram.

Father John Carroll said Hausa tribesmen "surprised" Igbos with an attack in Gombe on June 4, a Saturday. The Igbos fled to the train station. That night the local Emir or city chief, told them that no more trouble would occur and to return home. But the next day, "the rioting broke out again." A Catholic church and mission school were burned.

"Some 3,000 Ibos are now camped about the railway station hoping to find transportation southward. The mission fears that further outbreaks of violence are inevitable if the police leave the area," read the memo.

Catholic Bishop Lawton of Sokoto, who had been in Nigeria since 1954, met with Northern Nigeria's Military Governor Hassan Katsina, on June 3. He asked for 50 soldiers to restore confidence, according to a confidential U.S. Department of State telegram.

He asked Katsina for transportation to evacuate the "terrified Ibos" and "military escorts for safety purposes."

The governor's assistant, Liman Cirona, replied that he wanted to "avoid official involvement in movement of persons out of the north for fear such activity might give impression that it [was] official govt policy to evacuate southern element from north."

Lawton then told Cirona that the damaged churches require extensive repair for which the church could not pay. He asked for compensation for the Igbo people.

Liman "replied that compensation [was] not likely." He based his position of an earlier disturbance in Ibadan in the Western Region when rioting destroyed property and government compensation was not forthcoming for repairs.

Chapter 3

Some Igbos Flee from the North, Others Decide to Stay

An undetermined number of Igbos fled from Northern Nigeria after the May and June killings.

When surviving Igbos gathered at the Zaria train station, seeking the safest way to the Eastern Region, the American faculty at Ahmadu Bello University decided to feed them—and did so for several days.

The chief cook was Mary Futrell, who prepared meals in her university lab with food purchased in the local market. "We cooked up vegetables…a kind of typical Nigerian dish with peppers," she remembered. "We took it over to the train station."

She said that her husband took photographs of the train, but not the passengers on it, concerned that photographing surviving Igbos might get him in trouble with the authorities.

Whether this was the train or it was another train from the North, missionaries reported hearing that trains were stopped and Igbo passengers were killed.

The Disturbances

When one missionary heard that a train had been ambushed out of Zaria, Don Reece, a Baptist missionary in the Eastern Region, went out of curiosity to Enugu, the capital of the East. He wanted to confirm that what he had heard was true.

"I saw the havoc that had been wrought…Adults with swollen bodies that had begun to stink…The children that…had not been killed in the ambush were still on the train. The call went out if any of the Igbos anywhere…had relatives in the North they should come and see if they could find out who their children were, who these children belong to," said Reece.

What he witnessed shook him. Other missionaries expressed alarm at what they were hearing and seeing.

Roger Ingold, field secretary for the Church of the Brethren, sent a memorandum on June 2 to Henry Long, the general secretary of the Church of the Brethren mission headquartered in the United States.

"I have had eye-witness reports from Kaduna and Zaria. It appears that the press has been playing down the extent and severity of the demonstrations, rioting and damage done," he wrote. "The report is that many hotels and buildings owned by Ibos have been destroyed and it seems that there has been considerably more loss of life than has been reported."

Ingold wrote in longhand a note on the typed memo, asking that his paper only be shared verbally. "Jos is rumored listed for tomorrow. Tension has mounted."

Nothing happened in Jos, however. The rumors were false. Yet rumors became more and more prevalent as the months unfolded. Missionaries heard them from their Nigerian friends and colleagues.

On June 9, a Nigerian newspaper reported that the Head of the National Military Government and Supreme Commander of the Nigerian Armed

Forces, Major-General Johnson Aguiyi-Ironsi, had set up a commission to probe "the causes of the recent disturbances."

Aguiyi-Ironsi was an Igbo and had come to power after the January coup. His move to establish a commission was no doubt with the hopes of stemming the flow of Igbos to the East and reassuring the remaining Igbos in the North of their security.

Another Igbo leader, the military governor of Eastern Nigeria—Chukwuemeka Odumegwu Ojukwu—encouraged Igbos to return to the North.

"The May massacres of the Igbos—that the Igbos claimed that 3,000 people were killed—arising from the decree that declared Nigeria" a unitary state was "the final clincher in the argument that Igbos had planned to dominate Nigeria. That massacre didn't cause the Igbos to leave Nigeria. Ojukwu actually convinced and plead with the Igbos to go back to Northern Nigeria and to demonstrate that the Igbos had no bad intentions," said historian Godfrey Uzoigwe, a Nigerian, who has taught at the University of Michigan and Mississippi State University for many years.

Uzoigwe said Ironsi's Decree 34 centralized the government. Northern leaders opposed that move. They saw it as evidence of the Igbos' intention to run the country, an argument which Uzoigwe vigorously rejected.

Perhaps as a goodwill gesture, Ojukwu made the emir (chief) of Kano, a Hausa, the chancellor of the University of Nsukka. When the emir came to Nsukka for his installation, "he promised Ojukw and others that the Igbo would be safe. So, they went back," said Uzoigwe.

Igbos were uncertain about what to do. Many who had fled eastward had had their businesses looted or destroyed. But not all did.

The Disturbances

Elva Cowley wrote the Southern Baptist Convention's Foreign Mission Board on June 16 about a letter she had received from her son, Bill, principal at the Baptist High School in Jos.

She asked if the board had received news about "the disturbances." She shared that her son assured her that he and his family were in no danger in Jos, even though he also said that there were rumors that Jos would experience troubles.

"Bill said they discussed whether they should give their students and teachers who are from the East an opportunity to leave, but they and all others wished to stay and stick it out together whatever might come. Bill and Audrey [her daughter in-law] were touched by the demonstration of mature faith," she wrote.

Church of the Brethren missionary Ivan Eikenberry also wrote to mission executive Henry Long. He, in turn, distributed parts of this letter in a memo on July 22 to five key Church of the Brethren leaders. Long requested that they not use Eikenberry's name and to use the "information with great care."

"Reportedly, the northern Hausa Emirs (chiefs) have issued appeals to the Ibo people who fled, asking them to return and promising them safety and protection," wrote Eikenberry, who was then on furlough in the United States.

He wrote that "Zaria, Kano, Sokoto, Gusau were among the places where most violence occurred."

"Our steward's letter received today reported that a great number of Ibo have left Kaduna and other cities of the north," said Eikenberry.

Noting another source, he cited the "terrible conditions in the train stations as masses of Ibo people tried to travel southward from the northern cities. Both Protestant and Catholic Christians joined in trying to provide some food and assistance for those people, especially children and infants."

Enough Igbos had been killed or exited the North that critical services were disrupted.

Eikenberry pointed out that the Yola mail service had been interrupted. "In traveling we have to carry extra petrol along because there are few places where we formerly bought petrol that are closed and the people have 'run off,'" he wrote.

More often than not, Igbos had owned and operated the gas stations, which were now vandalized and some burned. Igbos had run the post offices, managed the airports, held banking positions, and occupied administrative positions in corporations—opportunities their education had afforded them.

Those who did not flee to the Eastern Region had clearly decided to trust the federal government and the traditional leadership of Northern Nigeria. For many, the North was their home. They had lived there for years. Their children had been born in the Hausa tribal land. They had good jobs. They owned businesses.

One family that decided to stay was the Ikerionwus. They had lived in Bukuru, a town about 10 miles from Jos, for some two decades, having moved there from the Eastern Region. Mr. Ikerionwu started off as a cook at the Amalgamated Tin Mining Company of Nigeria before moving to its headquarters. Their eldest son also worked for the company.

Their son, Jonathan, had been born in Bukuru in 1948. He was a student at the Baptist High School.

One of his classmates was Timothy Olagbemiro, whose father was a prominent Yoruba businessman.

When he lived in Bukuru at another boarding school, his scoutmaster was Ikerionwu's uncle—Mr. Illow. He held a senior position in the tin mining company. That Boy Scout troop was made up of Igbos, Yorubas and Hausas, said Olagbemiro.

While Olagbemiro was born in the Yoruba quarters of Jos, his father had built a new home in the Igbo quarters. "Igbos were my best friends," he said. He played soccer with them almost every day. Since the Olagbemiro family kept the team jerseys and balls, they had many Igbo boys in their home.

Olagbemiro lived and played with the Igbos. Yet his Christian family had intermarried with Muslims. Next door to the Yoruba Baptist Church was a mosque for Yorubas who had come to live in the North. Muslims went to the Christmas festival; Christians attended the Muslims festivals. The Christian and Muslim boys played soccer inside the mosque, chuckled Olagbemiro.

"Yorubas and Igbos were friends. Yorubas and Hausas were friends. But Hausas and the Igbos were not too close because they worked for them," he explained. The relationship between Igbos and Hausas was akin to "a master servant relationship."

In 1961, both Olagbemiro and Ikerionwu enrolled in the first class at the Baptist High School, a year after Nigeria had received its independence.

"Baptist High School is one of the best secondary schools…The buildings were excellent, were fantastic…Initially all the teachers in that school were missionaries from the United States. And they developed such a rapport—Christian way of living to the extent that we all took on that particular way of living. It was excellent," bragged Ikerionwu.

In a class of 30, he remembered being the only Igbo. His other classmates were mostly Yoruba with a few other tribal groups. They lived and worked together without "any tribal sentiment," he said. "That school was completely devoid of any tribal sentiment."

Neither he nor Olagbemiro personally knew one another at the start of the school year. But they had a family connection via the Boy Scout troop in Bukuru. They were joined by schoolboys from other tribes. One was a Fulani, the son of an influential Jos judge, said Olagbemiro.

"We regarded ourselves as our brother's keeper. We did things together… It was great," said Ikerionwu. To this day, his classmates still consider one another brothers.

His knowledge of several different languages probably enhanced his friendships with those of different tribes. He spoke English, Igbo, Yoruba and Hausa. "At one stage, I spoke Hausa better than Igbo."

Ikerionwu's attendance at the Baptist High School shaped his life. He credited the Cowleys, who "brought us up in the Christian way of doing things."

That approach was embedded in the school's motto—"Light and Life."

"We had to be light in our society, in our country. Wherever we are, we have to show examples to live in such a way that we make others to come to Christ. That is the essence of Baptist High School," he said.

Six years after starting school, atrocities and looting struck in May. A second military coup occurred in July.

Like other Igbos in Bukuru, the Ikerionwus surely witnessed the steady movement of anxious Igbos on trains to the East.

Robert Martenson wrote, "For weeks after my arrival at the Theological College of Northern Nigeria in Bukuru, I watched the trains as they headed south from Jos to Enugu, the capital of the eastern region. Several times a day they went through the city. They were loaded not with tin but rather with beds, household furnishings, and frightened families who were leaving jobs, homes, and possessions to return to safety in the land of their relatives."

Trains, however, became fewer and fewer—even as more and more Igbos camped out at the Bukuru station.

"I was frightened. My family in Burkuru were equally frightened," said Ikerionwu. They knew what had happened—two military coups, the May massacres, tribal accusations, rising tensions—and were anxious about what might happen next.

Apprehensive about Jonathan's well being, his oldest brother came to the high school to meet with Bill Cowley about his brother's safety.

"Dr. Cowley reassured him that I was in good hands. That they would look after me, take care of me," he remembered. The principal said if he wanted to go to the East, he could go.

"Personally I wanted to go. But when Dr. Cowley gave him [his older brother] the assurance that I would be in safe hands," he decided to stay. However, he did worry about the openness of the school campus in which Hausas in the surrounding village could easily enter.

Bill Cowley recalled the visit by Jonathan's older brother in mid-September. "The older brother came to the school to talk about Jonathan's future," especially concerned about troubles for the Eastern people, he said. "I told the brother that the choice was his, theirs, the families. If they wanted to take him home that was certainly their prerogative. Or if they wanted to leave him at school, we would do the best we could for him. We couldn't promise anything, but we would do the best we could to keep him safe. That was the agreement."

What would happen next would test the scriptural basis for the school: "Behold, how good and pleasant it is for brethren to dwell together in unity" (Psalm 133:1).

Chapter 4

Uncertainties and Tensions Escalate

"We have no reason to believe that the situation is serious. Everyone there and here is cautious and alert," wrote the Brethren mission general secretary Henry Long on July 22, reflecting a guarded optimism.

His optimism was not without concern. He did note that Nigeria had unrest in the North and cited a lengthy letter from Ivan Eikenberry about what had happened earlier.

Other mission agencies and missionaries had a shared optimism. They felt the situation was stable.

Meanwhile, the Lutheran Church-Missouri Synod mission board sent a missionary to northern Nigeria.

Fresh out of college, 23-year-old Carl Eisman, from New Albany, Indiana, arrived at the Jos Airport on July 23. He had a two-year assignment to teach at the interdenominational missionary boarding school, Hillcrest.

"We landed in Jos and there were people lined up all around the fence. There was a military guard. There was a band. And I looked out the window of the plane and said to myself, 'Wow, those missionaries really know how to welcome somebody,'" he said.

Inside the terminal, he discovered otherwise. People pushed him aside. Another plane had just landed with Major-General Ironsi, head of the Nigerian government.

"And that was what all the fanfare was for," said Eisman, who stood near the general as he was widely welcomed at the airport.

"I was impressed. He was a military man...He postured himself in every way that one would say, 'Wow this is the leader of the country'...I was very impressed," Eisman recalled.

Eisman was unaware at that time that Ironsi was an Igbo.

A week later, a newspaper headline ran, "Nigeria's Leader Seized in Mutiny."

A follow-up article in *The New York Times* noted, "The uprising by Nigerian Army insurgents reflects the mounting dissatisfaction of younger southerners in and out of the army with Maj. Gen. Johnson T. U. Aguiyi Ironsi."

Dusk-to-dawn curfews were established. Air traffic was grounded. A new government quickly emerged with the naming of a supreme commander. He was a Northerner, although not a Hausa, but an Angas. He was a Christian. He was trained at the UK's Royal Military Academy Sandhurst. He was 32 years old. His name was Lt. Col. Yakubu Gowan. "Gentleman Jack" would become his nickname.

In power, he announced that Ironsi had been kidnapped and his whereabouts unconfirmed.

Nigeria had undergone its second coup d'etat in 1966.

"All missionaries are safe," said Earl Fine in a memorandum on August 3 to his fellow Baptist missionaries with the subject line, "Recent Nigerian Disturbances."

"The Kano and Lagos airports were reopened yesterday after being closed for five days," he added, sharing that the United States Consulate had asked all Americans to restrict their travel.

Brethren missionaries Mark and Anita Keeney wrote on August 10 to Mark's mother in Bethel, Pennsylvania: "The trouble is all between different tribes, each wants to overlord over the other."

Reassuring her not to worry about them, they encouraged her to visit them in Nigeria for several months.

Another letter to the United States on August 13 spelled out in detail what had taken place across northern Nigeria.

"The latest trouble…was northerners killing Ibos. There is no telling how many have been killed," read the unsigned letter to "Evelyn" found in the Sudan Interior Mission archives. The letter asked that the contents not be repeated and published.

Missionaries in the Sokoto province were evacuated. Two theological students in the rural town of Kaltungo were killed with machetes. SIM bookshops in Katsina and Gusau "were practically demolished. Ibos in Raham were killed and their houses burned. The Baptist missionaries in Kantagora were evacuated…People lived at the railway stations all over the North trying to get back East," read the letter.

"Eventually things seemed to quiet down. All Ibos came back to Jos offices and bookshop; they reopened canteens, etc.," the letter said.

Brethren field secretary Ingold's August 31 memo to Henry Long reported on the country's instability but the security of the missionaries. He said, "300,000 Ibo refugees are now in the Eastern region."

After thanking Long for building confidence among American family members, he wrote, "I need to share a concern that I now have, that we somehow also convey the idea that in the present Nigeria, in Africa, yes, in the world in which we live, we are not free from danger. Nor do I feel that we should hold this high as an objective. It does seem to be part of the calling of a Christian worker or missionary…[T]here is an element of danger in the world in which we live. I'm reminded that there was in the world in which Christ lived. It was faced by the New Testament Church and we need to indicate, that as Christians, we face the world and the future courageously."

Ingold included with his memo a letter from the Nigerian Consultation of Christian Laity, formed a few weeks earlier and signed by Mrs. Rosa Ademola.

Dated September 1, the letter called on Christians to work for peace and national unity.

"Some of Nigeria's immediate problems were clearly tribal," the letter recorded. "Most of all, the present national situation was seen as reflecting the failure of God's Church in Nigeria to make real in the life of the nation His Gospel of peace and love."

My parents, Baptist missionaries Bob and Jo Ann Parham, sent a September 13 letter to their United States friends: "For years it [Nigeria] was considered the most stable country in Africa. So it is difficult for us to understand what is taking place now."

Their uncertainty about what was taking place had not led to a withdrawal into pessimism. They shared how thrilled they were that Bob Parham's parents had visited them in the summer.

I remember meeting my grandparents at the Lagos airport and traveling for several days to Jos. There were four adults and five children in our blue Peugeot station wagon. We drove through the Western Region to the Jebba Bridge, one of two single-lane bridges across Nigeria's two major rivers—the Niger and the Benue. Both bridges handled vehicles and rail traffic, as well as the flow of pedestrians and livestock. From Jebba, we went to Kaduna and then home to Jos.

Another Baptist missionary, Homer Brown, said in a September 27 letter to H. C. Goerner, general secretary for Africa at the Foreign Mission Board in Richmond, Virginia, "Conditions in Nigeria are much the same as they have been. There is tension that one can feel where ever you go…We are…fervently praying for peace and harmony."

Missionaries were hearing rumors and knew about outbreaks of localized conflict. They were praying for peace. They and Nigerian Christian leaders hoped for a positive future after so much political turmoil and violence earlier in the year. Yet none could predict what was about to happen.

Chapter 5

Tensions Crest

Missionaries felt the tension building in late September.

Some witnessed tribal outbreaks in mid-September. Two who did were the Kiekovers, Christian Reformed Church missionaries.

Harvey and Thelma Kiekover had arrived in Nigeria in November 1965. Their first task was six months of language study. Their first assignment was urban evangelism in Makurdi, a small town on the Benue River that functionally divided the Hausa North and the Igbo East, although it was located in the Tiv tribal area.

Depending on road conditions, Makurdi was a five- to six-hour drive from Jos, heading North, and three hours to Enugu, heading South.

Distinct from the Hausa tribe, the Tiv preferred their own language to that of Hausa.

"The Tiv were more similar to the Igbo than to the Hausa people, but they belong to the North because it was located in what was then known as the Northern Region," said Harvey Kiekover.

Makurdi had a one-lane, half-mile long bridge across the Benue River. It handled both trains and vehicles—all movement of people North and South.

On September 21, "the first eruption of violence took place," recalled Kiekover.

That morning, a mallam (a Muslim religious teacher) came to the Kiekovers' home about two miles from town to help them learn Hausa.

"He came and said, 'Terrible things are happening in the town.' And we knew nothing about it…[He] described a little bit of what was happening in terms of the killing of Igbos," said Kiekover. "While he was talking to us, our steward's wife, Rebecca, came back crying, deeply, deeply troubled. And she said, 'Things are happening in town that are too bad to talk about.'"

It was mainly the soldiers that were killing the Igbo people, he said. "I don't think there were many Tiv people involved in that."

"We became very concerned about Oko, our yard boy…Oko was an Igbo. So we were very frightened and uncertain about what to do. I can still see his eyes wide with fright…It was Linus [the Kiekovers' steward, who was married to Rebecca], this Christian Tiv man, who said, 'It's not safe to go into the town. But there is a way through the field from here to the railway station.'"

Kiekover remembered that Linus said, "I can take Oko to the railway station…Hopefully a train will come…and evacuate [him] from Makurdi to his Eastern Region."

That plan seemed the best way to get Oko to safety, said Kiekover. "I didn't know what to do. We had only been in Makurdi for about four months. And were new to the town."

The Kiekovers purchased Oko's bicycle and gave him some traveling money. Linus took him to the train station and returned two hours later. At six o'clock that evening, they were relieved when they heard the train whistle.

"About three weeks later…we got a note from him. He arrived safely… But he had been robbed by soldiers by gunpoint [in the Eastern Region]," said Kiekover. "And that's the last we ever heard from him."

To the east of Makurdi was the village of Zaki Biam, where matters were also grim for the Igbos.

Zaki Biam had a flourishing market with a number of Igbo citizens.

Hearing rumors of impending violence, many Igbos in Zaki Biam packed up their belongings and took flight across the Cameroon border. Others stayed in the village. Those who did suffered the consequences for either their deep trust in their fellow Nigerians, or their horrible denial of the danger.

When the military and police arrived, they rounded up as many Igbos as they could, executing them with gunshot.

The next morning after widespread killing, a Tiv pastor came to the home of Christian Reformed Church missionary Lee Baas. Baas had arrived in Nigeria in 1965. His assignment was mobile evangelism—showing Christian films in the Tiv tribal language.

The Tiv pastor made an odd request, even for one who was new to Nigeria. He invited Baas to see his field, his farm. There, Baas found that Tiv elders and church members had hidden Igbos. They told him that that night the Igbos would be taken to his home. He would transport them to the Cameroons—to safety.

"I had a very small Opel…We got 13 adults" in the vehicle, he said. "We couldn't take everyone." At midnight, he drove them to safety. The next night the same trip was repeated. This time, however, they had to evade a police roadblock. Seeing the barricade, Baas faked a turn at a fork in the road and accelerated down the other one.

"I've never heard silence so loud as when the people saw the police. They knew I would have to stop and they would be killed," said Baas.

"It is traumatic to tell [about the trips] because I know there were people who didn't make it," said Baas. Missionaries did what they could. "Missionaries who were there front and center didn't duck their responsibility."

Some of the rescued Igbos returned years later to thank Baas. One was a young man who recalled that when he was 4 years old, Baas had driven him and his parents across the border to the sanctuary of the Cameroons.

What was happening in Tiv land filtered out across Nigeria.

"We heard rumors that Igbos were killed in outlying stations," said John Price, a high school student at Hillcrest, whose parents were with the Sudan Interior Mission.

He wrote in his diary on September 24 about returning from "canteen," a weekend social event for Hillcrest high school students held at ELM House hostel, and encountering a soldier.

"The first sign of things going bad in Jos were when we got stopped going back from canteen one night by an army guy who was speaking erratically and didn't seem to know what he was talking about from my perspective," wrote Price.

"In Nigeria, there was always something brewing...always a great tribal rivalry," observed then 23-year-old Beverly Knuth. She had arrived as a Lutheran Church-Missouri Synod missionary in Nigeria in 1965 and moved to Jos to teach at Hillcrest. She also served as an assistant houseparent at ELM House in the fall of 1966.

"I didn't know that anything terribly different was going to be happening," she said. But in late September, "we were told not to let the students go into town. We were to keep them close, keep them at the hostel."

On September 27, she wrote to her mother and father: "The trouble within the country is far from settled and most of the people feel something may blow up on Saturday...There has been no trouble up here but I can imagine something could happen. There are road blocks up around Jos and they check all lorries and taxis that come in and out of town...We hear so many stories these days about the situation that you really don't know what to believe."

On the same day, Baptist missionary Homer Brown wrote to H. C. Goerner about the widespread tensions.

Christian Reformed Church missionary Harry Boer especially felt the tensions. He was the principal at the Theological College of Northern Nigeria in Bukuru, some 10 miles from Jos.

Boer even approached an Igbo friend, a tailor, named Sunday, urging him to join the exodus of Igbos. Sunday refused, saying, "I came to the North to work, I have a job to do, and I'm going to keep on working."

By September 27, Sunday had changed his mind, sensing the growing tension. He told Boer, "I'm going home on the next train."

"Everywhere there was a feeling that more and worse was to come," wrote Boer. "On the evening of the 28th I sat in my office to prepare for the next day's teaching, but I could concentrate on nothing. There was in me a feeling of great uncertainty, a sense of something horrible impending."

He witnessed earlier that afternoon hundreds of Igbos "crowded together" at the railway station, waiting for the next train. He had seen Sunday among them.

"I decided to go to Jos to see Rev. [Edgar] Smith…He had many connections, perhaps he could reassure me. But I found him as troubled and perplexed as I was," wrote Boer, in *History of the Theological College of Northern Nigeria, 1950-1971* (1983).

On his return drive to Bukuru, Boer gave two soldiers a lift. "They were on the way to do duty at a road-block about a half mile south of the Hillcrest school. As I dropped them off, one of them said, 'Go back to your school, bature [white man], and stay there. Tomorrow there will be big trouble.'"

Their warning was surely understated given what would happen.

Chapter 6

It Has Started

By the time Boer returned to Bukuru, matters had deteriorated badly.

"When I entered Bukuru there was already trouble afoot. There was excited shouting in town, there was banging on doors and there were cries that I could not understand. A short little man ran across the street with a suitcase in his hand and disappeared into the shadows. Doubtless, he was seeking refuge at the railway station," wrote Boer.

Theological College of Northern Nigeria students met him. They were fearful. They asked him to turn off the floodlights that illuminated the chapel tower, making it visible for miles around at night.

Boer told the students not to be fearful. He said the light would remain on, and that anyone who sought refuge on the campus would be received.

The clamor from the town continued until after midnight.

A faculty member at the Theological College of Northern Nigeria, Robert Martenson, wrote one of the few published articles about what happened.

"On the night of September 28th the peace which the Jos-Buruku area had enjoyed came to an end. Screams in the night told of death. Loud pounding on wooden doors announced the entrance of an angry mob into another Ibo home or store, in an attempt to dislodge every Ibo from the area," he wrote.

"By morning there were many dead bodies in the ditches, woods and streets of Bukuru. The only ones who escaped violence that night were those who had camped on the train station platform, still hoping that a train would be coming soon to take them away from the danger."

Meanwhile, five miles outside the city of Jos, late that night, the phone rang at the Baptist High School's principal's home, an oddity given how seldom phones worked in Nigeria.

"At 1:00 a.m. or 2:00 a.m., the phone rang, picked it up, the first words we heard was, 'It has started,'" said Baptist missionary Bill Cowley.

The caller was Archie Dunaway. Archie and Margaret Dunaway were house parents at the Baptist Hostel, located at the outskirts of Jos, not far from the market.

"We knew immediately what it was, that the rumors were now fulfilled, that there was action. We could hear in the background the sounds of people screaming, running, people being beaten, all sorts of horrific sounds. We knew it had started," said Cowley.

The Hausas were orchestrating the attack on the Igbos. They had an organization, believed Cowley, "that they had been working on for months at least. That was to identify all of the Eastern people in whatever given area—who are they, where do they live, what are they doing. So that at a moment's notice they could call on that information and if they wanted to drive the people out, they knew where to find them."

Cowley said, "The driving out was by killing. Driving out had occurred previously...Some people—who were apprehensive—went back to the East and stayed just there. Some people had never even been in the East. They were Easterners, but they had been born in the North. They may be second or third generation in the North. But still had their Eastern identity."

Some Igbos had decided to stay in the North, thinking they would be safe. Others had returned North after evacuating several months earlier.

Across town from the Baptist High School, Dean and Glenis Petersen, missionaries with Sudan United Mission who had arrived at Hillcrest School in December 1962, had their own phone call.

"The night it happened in Jos we can ever well remember. We had visitors in. They went home about 10 or 10:30 at night. And it wasn't much longer that the phone began ringing. And they told us that the trouble had started in Jos. And we listened out the windows. We could hear dogs barking and screaming at people. Just a clamor from town. And we lived about a mile and half out of town," remembered Dean Petersen.

Their evening guests had to go through Jos to reach their home. They called to warn the Petersens of what was happening.

"It was very close to midnight...and I heard the gun shots and the squeals and the yelling and the running of people. At first, I thought okay, 'What's going on outside, maybe they are chasing a wild animal or something.' Then I looked out the window and saw the mob," recalled Ruth Keeney, a Hillcrest high school senior.

Keeney had lived in Nigeria for almost a decade. She was seasoned in her understanding of the country. The Keeneys had arrived in Nigeria in 1957. Upon their arrival, they dropped Ruth off at Hillcrest for the start of the school year. Her parents moved to a bush station without electricity and with a kerosene refrigerator. Her father did evangelistic work.

The street lights illumined what she witnessed in front of Boulder Hill, the hostel for the Church of the Brethren, about a quarter of a mile closer to town than Hillcrest School and across the street from the governor's compound.

Keeney turned off her room light, deciding that the mob would quickly pass and she would continue to study with a flashlight.

"It did not stop," she said. Other students woke up. The hostel lights remained off.

"You heard the whacking. We knew they were being beaten in the grass," said Keeney.

Boulder Hill house parent Buzz Bowers recalled, "We heard noise out on the street…we could see people running in the direction of the Hillcrest School, carrying things. And they had been looting the Igbo houses. And I remember seeing [someone] carrying a sewing machine."

As violence blanketed Jos, Bill and Audrey Cowley had a sleepless night. They were worried about their Eastern faculty members and Igbo students. They "rolled over in their minds" what their options were.

"What could we do, what should we do?" said Cowley, explaining the crisis that he and Audrey faced. "Options were limited. We…couldn't build that fortress around the school. We still had to carry on day to day. But there was one thing that was very prominent in our minds at that point. We had a few students and a few teachers who were of Eastern origin. They lived at the school. They were part of the school life. But we were quite sure that everybody nearby at least knew that they were there. We felt really vulnerable at that point. And what could we do?"

The school was located in the Hausa village of Naraguta. Given the traffic between those at the school and the villagers, the Hausas knew the tribal makeup of the Baptist High School.

The Cowleys knew that going to the school campus and raising the alarm would be a mistake. They decided to "sit real tight until daylight and then put into operation a plan."

"The plan we came to was that we should try to hide those few teachers and students until we could come up with some plan to get them safely out. And the plan we came to was to bring them to the compound where we lived which was about a mile from the school. It happened on that compound that there was an empty house…We could put them in this house and keep it locked up."

Their plan, however, had a likely stumbling block. Their gardener was a man named Garba. He was a Hausa. He was "furiously Muslim to the point that he didn't ever want to hear the name Jesus. He didn't want any directions, instructions from a woman…Now we're bringing into his territory, so to speak, these Eastern people," said Cowley. "Was it prudent to bring them there knowing that he was there and could very quickly raise the alarm and do them in?…So we had to think about him."

Audrey Cowley agreed with her husband. She knew Garba had a deep prejudice against the Igbos, a prejudice not based on skin pigmentation like in the United States, but tribalism.

The tribal prejudice "was not totally the fault of the Hausas. The Igbos were very prideful. They were educated. They had good jobs. And they let it be known that they were well educated and had good jobs. This did not stand well with the Hausas, who were not well educated and did not have good jobs. They were jealous, but they were also angry because the Igbos were so prideful," she said.

Bill Cowley told Garba what they were planning to do. Then, he added that they could not do that unless they had his word that he would protect the Easterners.

"Garba didn't answer immediately. He went off to think about it…I could tell he was struggling," recalled Cowley. Cowley reminded Garba that it was Eastern people who had kindly helped his wife get medical treatment in order to conceive a child.

Garba returned with his answer: "I won't do it for them…But I'll do it for you."

"I knew him well enough to know that with all the problems we had that he was a person of honor. And if he said he would protect, he would protect, which he did," remembered Cowley.

Cowley then went to the school and told those of Eastern origin to get quietly into the vehicle. They followed his instructions, albeit without knowing his plan.

"We brought the six men and boys over and kept them in the house for several days until we could determine what to do next. We told them to keep the blinds drawn, to be quiet. We would feed them, but they were not to reveal their presence," remembered Audrey Cowley.

Yoruba student Timothy Olgabemiro said that the other Baptist High School students didn't know what had happened to the disappearing Easterners.

"None of us knew. They did it so perfectly well…Nobody knew until after they were gone…Nobody knew of this way which the missionaries tried to actually assist our students and staff," he recalled.

The violence in the North had profound consequences in the West, the Yoruba tribal area.

On Friday, September 30, Keith Edwards, a medical missionary at the Baptist hospital in Ogbomosho, located in the Yoruba heartland, wrote in his diary about what he felt and had heard.

"If an instrument could be made to measure tension, like a thermometer measures heat, such an instrument would have a high reading today," he wrote. "Police and soldiers are reported guarding Jebba bridge, Lagos, Ikeja, the airport, and so forth. There was fighting in Jos yesterday. Rumors coming down from there now say that it was 'ransacked.' Thirty-five or more people (mostly Easterners) have been killed at Kainji dam, and all construction there has stopped."

Edwards wrote about an official with the United States' A.I.D, who had stopped near Kaduna. Smelling an odor, he walked into a field where he counted 85 dead soldiers in a field.

"On Friday we heard rumors that there were troubles and killings at Kainji Dam," he wrote. The next day "10 to 12 huge lorries" from the Kainji Dam "came through Ogbomosho and refueled here. They were loaded with about 1000 or more people some of whom were wounded. It was a pitiful sight with people crowded so close together in the lorries that they could not sit down."

Upon hearing of the injured, Edwards went to the gas station to see if he could help. He told them he was a doctor. They turned down his offer, preferring to leave as soon as they had refueled.

Given the reports and rumors, the hospital's executive committee scheduled a meeting to talk about "telling all Easterners on our staff that they are free to go home." They would also be assured that they could return to their jobs in a few months if things were calm.

Chapter 7

Hiding the Igbos

As Bill and Audrey Cowley were hiding Igbo faculty members and students, surviving Igbos were fleeing for any possible place of protection from marauding Hausa gangs with machetes, hoes and clubs.

One man ran into my seventh-grade classroom at Hillcrest School before a spelling test. He was sweating profusely. He was wide-eyed. His clothing was dirty, tattered.

He was an Igbo.

Classmate Dean Gilliland recalled the man running into the room being "very afraid."

"Please ma, I don't want to die," he said to our teacher, Miss Wagner, an Assemblies of God missionary.

Lutheran missionary Carl Eisman had seen him dash across campus only a few minutes earlier.

"As the physical education teacher, I was outside on the basketball courts. And I remember seeing a Nigerian man running across the compound above the basketball courts into one of the classrooms. He was yelling and screaming," said Carl Eisman. "He was fleeing for his life. You could hear it in his voice."

"The riots had broken out in the early hour of the morning," said Wagner. "We could hear a few gun shots, but there weren't many guns being used…We were well-aware that in the Igbo section of our town things were beginning to happen. We had no idea, of course, of the extent of what might happen."

She had gone on to school that morning, maintaining a sense of normalcy.

"I caught out of the corner of my eye a single man coming up from the road, the main road past Hillcrest school. I could tell easily by his build that he was an Igbo. It seemed very obvious to me that he was running away from something. And I was concerned because my door was right in line with the direction he was going. I was responsible for a classroom of wonderful people, entrusted to my care…I really did not want that man coming in there. But he did come in," said Wagner.

She immediately met him. "I said to him, 'You can't stay in this room.' And he said to me, 'But madam, I don't want to die. I don't want to die.'"

I knew trouble was in the air with all the coups and the riots in Zaria. Little did I know, however, that this unnamed Igbo, who ran into our room, was a messenger whose panic was evidence of the unfolding violence in Jos and across Northern Nigeria.

I didn't learn until five decades later what Ms. Wagner did. Nor did I connect this man's death with what my father did early the next morning.

Our teacher quickly escorted him out of the room toward the principal's office in an adjacent building, where high school students attended class. She was worried about the safety of her students and concerned about the man's welfare. She guided him across open ground between the two buildings. When he spotted a group of workers, he left her side to talk to them.

"I suppose he felt comfortable with them. At least they were not out among the rioters and assumed them to be friendly," said Wagner. She returned to her classroom, thinking he was in good hands.

"I was to learn later that those men told him that he would find his best security, up in the rocks behind Hillcrest School," she recalled.

Jos was littered with oval-shaped granite boulders of varying sizes. Some were the size of a bathtub. Others were the size of an extra-large SUV. Still others were larger than multi-storied office buildings. Often smaller boulders sat precariously atop larger ones. Grayish boulders leaned on one another, providing crawl spaces and caverns.

We had a formation in our backyard with a small but unmovable egg-shaped rock balancing on top of a larger one. In the fissure between them, one day we found a three-foot spitting cobra.

These rock formations became shelters for terrified Easterners across the plateau.

To get to the rock formation with caves and crevasses, the fleeing Igbo had to walk a short distance past the Assemblies of God rest home.

Enua, Wagner's steward, saw him and recognized his plight. Enua was a Northerner—not a Hausa. He was a Berum, a completely different tribe that had originally settled the Jos area. Enua took him to his house and fed him.

Described as a fine, responsible, Christian man, Enua then told the man where to hide in the rocks.

Later that afternoon, after supper, the man showed up at Wagner's kitchen door. He was "obsessed" with the idea of getting to the railway station. She discouraged him, knowing that he would not make it all the way through town with the roving gangs. She urged him to return to the rocks. "I told him again that his best security would be up in the rocks," said Wagner, who gave him a rug upon which to sleep.

A mile down the Bauchi Road on the way to the Jos Airport, the house parents at ELM House were deciding how best to protect their students—and their Igbo employees.

The ELM House staff were mostly Igbos, remembered Lutheran missionary and Hillcrest teacher Beverly Knuth. "They were people who had come up to ELM House because most of our missionaries at the time lived in their area," in the East. Having recognized different talents and training, the Eastern Region Lutheran missionaries had recommended their employment in Jos.

She relayed that their staff of eight to ten lived on the compound, many with their families.

"We had housing quarters behind the hostel," she said. "People around knew we had Igbo employees and they would be targeted…We felt there was danger."

"After hearing reports all day, piecemeal, coming in about what was happening in Jos, a mile and a half from Hillcrest, it was pretty horrible…The information filtered to us that there was wholesale slaughtering going on and that homes and businesses were being looted. Cars were torched. And it was definitely a tribe thing…Well, we had our Igbo staff," reported Eisman, who was also living at the hostel.

As soon as the Lutheran missionary children got home from school, Eisman and Knuth met with Paul and Margaret Griebel, ELM House's house parents. They put their heads together to decide what to do. They knew local Hausas were aware that they had Igbo employees. They were afraid that some Hausas would enter the ELM House compound harming both staff and missionary children.

"They were family," said Knuth about their Igbo staff. "They were part of your family. How could you not help them? I don't think there was any qualm at all about doing what we could to keep them safe. Nobody gave a second thought. That was the right thing to do."

The Griebels decided to move the 30 children for the night to Mountain View, the Christian Reformed Church hostel. It was nearer to Hillcrest. Eisman speculated that perhaps the Griebels thought that Mountain View would be safer since they believed it did not have an Igbo staff.

In fact, it did, said Nancy DeVries, the daughter of Dick and Cindy Devries, the house parents, who remembered that they were approached by an Igbo carpenter named Emmanuel. He had made furniture for her parents. He asked them to hide him—and they did. They hid him in the hostel's hot-water heater closet and later took him to the police station. She did not learn what her parents had done until years later.

When Emmanuel was hidden is unclear. Nonetheless, Margaret Griebel and Beverly Knuth accompanied the children with the intentions of returning to ELM House the next morning. Paul Griebel and Carl Eisman stayed with the Igbo employees.

"As the evening wore on…nothing had happened…We turned out all the lights. We locked all the doors. It seemed quiet outside. We could hear screaming going on from time to time," Eisman said. "Nothing was directed at us."

Eisman and Griebel went to bed—not for long, however. They heard noise in the driveway. They peeked through the windows from the darkened house.

"We could see figures in the night that were growing in number. We could see flashlights bobbing up and down. We could hear them first talking, then yelling, then screaming, almost like cheering. In a sense they were whipping themselves into a frenzy. That's when Paul and I knew that they were the Hausas that knew that there were Igbos inside," said Eisman.

The missionaries had hidden their Igbo staff and their families in a storage room inside the hostel, some in a large space and others in a crawl space above the ceiling.

"We assembled the Igbos…and put them in a rather large linen closet… It was right off of the main area where we would eat our meals…It had a door on it, but the door was covered with a draw curtain. So we felt it was the safest place for them to be, because it had no windows in the back," recalled Eisman. "We provided them with food. We provided them with water. We tried to make them as comfortable as we could…We would check on them… They were obviously frightened."

As the mob reached a fever pitch, Eisman said, "I'm standing in the shadows with my hunting knife. My knees were shaking. Paul is sitting at the table reading scripture" and praying.

Protecting an Igbo staff member was also a concern of Paul Weaver, the Hillcrest School principal. Weaver, a Church of the Brethren missionary, likely hid one of his office staff, a man named Hycenth Adibenma, although Weaver kept his actions secret.

Adibenma "was the secretary for Principal Weaver," said Wagner. "Much loved. I think the students and staff all enjoyed having Hycenth around…He was an Igbo and every Igbo in town was at risk."

"I heard two stories" on where Adibenma was hidden. "I had heard that Paul Weaver…had taken him into his house and had kept him in his attic… Then, I've also heard that he was kept up in the auditorium…In any case, Hillcrest kept his life."

Student Ruth Keeney, who volunteered in the school office, remembered that Adibenma was hidden in the rafters above the sanctuary or auditorium. She believed it was Weaver who had found him a hiding place.

Before chapel ended at Theological College of Northern Nigeria (TCNN) in Bukuru on the morning of September 29, Harry Boer, the principal and a Christian Reformed Church missionary, "forbade all students to leave campus without permission."

Students then adjourned for their classes—classes never started.

The TCNN students and staff saw Igbos "running out of the stand of young eucalyptus trees…Some came directly to the College, others scattered to other areas," wrote Boer.

Robert Martenson wrote, "We could see them coming across the open country that separated the railroad station from the college. Soon we were confronted by scores of frightened human beings, pale with fear, asking what they should do…Some of the Ibos went into the vast bush country but many were inclined to stay near the college, hidden in a small mountain of boulders."

As the day continued, the gangs searched for and killed their enemies. The police did keep some of the mob away from the college "but it was easy to see that there was no law elsewhere in the land. On that day of violence a man could kill another without fear of punishment," said Martenson.

He wrote of a "shriveled-up man who came by night after spending the whole day submerged in a pond of muddy water; the man who came early the next day, asking for Communion so that he might be prepared to die."

Boer would learn later that the police had withdrawn from the train station where Igbos had gathered. "When they had left, rioters armed with clubs fell upon the Ibos and began beating to death all those whom they could reach. The others fled in terror."

A TCNN staff member, Karl Lundager, remembered seeing the Igbos fleeing toward the chapel "with the killers right on their heels. We saw rioters attacking, beating, slaughtering whoever they could get hold of."

The night before was a moonlit evening filled with "screams and shouting," Lundager said. As he and his wife, Bjorg, had stood outside the chapel bathed in light, listening to the alarming sounds, a young boy of 15, named Uche, ran to them. He told them what was happening in Bukuru, outside their campus. They took him to their kitchen—fed and prayed for him. Then, Lundager took the lad with a blanket into the rocks behind the school and hid him in a cave.

The next day, after treating six injured Igbos "with morphine and penicillin" in the school's dispensary, Mrs. Lundager took a medicine bag into the rocks where she found Uche.

He said to her, "When they come to kill me, please, tell them to kill me completely!"

She replied, "No! But I will kneel with you and ask God to help you."

That day, after two armed police officers appeared on campus, Boer rushed to Jos. He was seeking more officers to protect the 35 Igbos, who had sought refuge at the college. The Jos chief of police assigned 12 officers "armed with rifles" to guard the campus.

Missionaries were not the only ones hiding Igbos.

In a letter dated December 15, 1966, Priscilla Opara wrote to Doris Price, a missionary with the Sudan Interior Mission, who lived in Jos. She was the mother of Hillcrest student John Price.

Opara relayed to her Bible teacher and friend that she had fled in disguise and sought refuge in the home of a Northern family.

"I ran to a village 14 miles away from Jos with a taxi. I had to disguise in Yoruba attire and I stayed there in a friend's house, a Northerner…I did not know they will be kind not to kill women and I also remembered what happened to people who ran to the police station in Katsina during the first trouble," wrote Opara.

The Jos and Bukuru killings came a week after the killings the Kiekovers had experienced in Makurdi.

The Kiekovers were listening to the two-way radio broadcast from Sudan United Mission leader Edgar Smith when they heard the news about the plateau. Smith reported, "It is a very dark day in Jos."

That was Smith's "cryptic way of saying that now the violence had erupted in Jos. That was one week after it happened in Makurdi," said Kiekover.

The targeting of Ibgos was widespread in the North. Having hidden survivors, missionaries knew neither how long they could keep them safe, nor how they would get them to safety. That dynamic set off urgent scrambling.

Chapter 8

Second Night, Second Day in Jos

The killings continued in Jos into the second night and second day.

Standing in the shadows inside ELM House as the mob whipped themselves into a frenzy, Carl Eisman faced a moral crisis: What to do if the mob broke down the door and entered the hostel searching for the hidden Igbos?

"I was extremely confused as to what to do because what are the chances, what are the options? If they break down the door...which they could easily do en masse, I'm standing there with my hunting knife and I'm going, should I stand there and say, 'Okay you have to go over me and to get to them,' to protect them, knowing that in the frenzy they were in they would just kill me...Should I step aside because I'm not who they are after?" said Eisman.

"Where is my moral obligation? Where is my obligation as a Christian to other Christians who I know if I step aside these people are going to be murdered?" Eisman asked himself as Paul Griebel remained in prayer.

The outside frenzy peaked and then there was silence. Griebel and Eisman watched through the window as the crowd dispersed.

"It was an answer to some prayer. It certainly wasn't because Carl Eisman was standing there with his knife in his hand," he said. "Nothing happened the rest of the night."

Eisman wondered what had caused the mob to disperse. He got his answer the next morning. He saw a body in the driveway.

"There was a male body, a Nigerian male body who had been castrated… He had been beaten to death," recalled Eisman, concluding that the man had been running through the compound and ran into the mob.

Wanting to hide the body before the children returned to change clothes for school that day, Griebel and Eisman drug the body to a drainage ditch with elephant grass. They rolled him into the ditch and covered the body with a metal sheet.

The hidden Igbos remained in the linen closet, albeit exhausted from the frightful night.

Early that morning, Baptist missionary Bob Parham drove into downtown Jos to the city post office. He was looking for the safest route for Archie Dunaway to drive through town without the Baptist hostel's children seeing the dead bodies.

"He found a little boy on the steps of the post office who he had bought newspapers from who had been killed," remembered Jo Ann Parham. "I think there were nine bodies around a three block space and other dead bodies on the road."

Seeing problems deeper into town, Parham returned home and called the Dunaways, telling them to go a different route.

When Parham took his own children to Hillcrest, he found a dead body on the veranda of one of the buildings.

"He asked the children to stay in the car. He was looking for somebody who could help him transport that body to the morgue. He found a missionary, Dave McCauley, who was with Assemblies of God, who had a truck or a vehicle in which they could transport the body. So, they took him to the morgue," said Parham.

The identity of the deceased man was unknown to Parham, but perhaps not to Phyllis Wagner.

Ahead of school that morning, the Igbo who had run into her classroom the day before and whom she had told to hide in the rocks, came to her home. He was returning the rug she had given him. He told her he was going into town to the train station.

Wagner discouraged him from pursuing his plan. She knew that it was unsafe for him to take either one of two routes to the police compound—following the train tracks behind the school or walking through town. The man walked off.

"He got as far as the principal's office," she said, when he was confronted by men working on the campus. He ran back to her house.

The men followed him. "They stood under the flamboyant tree in my yard...One man had a machete...But they finally left," she said.

The Igbo man walked down to Hillcrest's driveway to get to the main road into town. As she walked to her classroom, Wagner saw him fleeing in her direction being chased by a gang of thugs.

Fifteen or 20 people carrying clubs and machetes pursued him. Wagner yelled at them.

"I watched them. They followed him. It was more, it seemed, like a sport. They knew they had their captive. There was no out for him at the point," she said. He ran across the school campus. They caught and killed him.

Missionary student Dean Gilliland said he witnessed from his dorm room in Maxwell Hall the gang chasing the man and striking him down.

"I learned later that…Robert Parham and Dave McCauley…picked up the body," said Wagner.

Timothy Olagbemiro, a Yoruba, whose Baptist family lived in the Igbo section of town, explained that his family was not in danger. The Hausas "knew him [his father]…But they came to the houses all around…A man was almost lynched in front of my father's house." His father took the man to the hospital.

Even at the hospital, Igbos were killed, said Olagbemiro. He shared that at one point he was even mistaken for an Igbo. Other Yorubas with tribal marking on their faces persuaded the Hausas that he was a Yoruba.

Writing a nine-page letter to his Sudan United Mission headquarters in London, Geoffrey Dearsley reported that on September 29 his Igbo carpenter, Lawrence, "staggered into the compound completely exhausted, reporting that all his property had been destroyed and we promptly hid him in the carpenter's store and very shortly after this a gang went by our entrance, but fortunately did not come in. Further gangs of people were seen streaming into Jos from various directions."

The Dearsleys were concerned about Lawrence's safety, fearing that a gang "might come and comb our compound."

Knowing of the Dearsleys' anxiety, Edgar and Nelle Smith arranged for him to stay in their home and secretly transported him to a safer location.

Dearsley contrasted the actions of the army with that of the police. He wrote that the gangs drove Igbos into groups who were then shot by the army. Police actions were far different.

"As far as we can gather, the Police were completely helpless in all this to do anything to prevent it, but whenever there was opportunity they seem to have helped, and everyone is very much praising them. They were able to steer off the gangs from the railway station and seal off a group of Ibos there and they also set up an enclosure at the Police Station where any who escaped there were safe."

High school student John Price lived with his parents across the street from the Sudan Interior Mission bookshop, one mile from Hillcrest and half-a-mile from the city market.

He wrote in his diary on September 29: "No school for me. The Northerners are killing Eboes and the police are protecting them and the army is helping the killers, so if the police and army fight, we have to scram."

While Price missed a day of school, the school remained in session. The faculty wanted to maintain as much normalcy as possible for younger students living in dorms on campus and older students living in the area hostels who could come into campus.

Principal Weaver later wrote in his school report about the fall's activities that the "school carried on as usual during the recent disturbances."

During the school day, Paul Griebel reported, "An additional army regiment had been sent to Jos to stabilize things. And that they had actually secured the Nigerian police compound….The word had gotten out…that Igbos…could be brought to the police compound," said Eisman. "I do not remember how he facilitated this, but Paul was able to get our Igbos…to the police compound."

Griebel and Eisman decided after school how to handle the dead body still in the drainage ditch.

"We had heard that one could get through the city. That they were digging mass graves on the other side of the city because so many people had been killed," said Eisman.

Eisman and Jim Dretke, another Lutheran missionary, determined to drive across town to take the body to the mass gravesite.

"I remember us pulling the vehicle in front of the body and blocking the view from the ELM House windows to the drainage ditch. We really couldn't lift the body up out of the drainage ditch in the van by ourselves. So two of the more mature high school students…helped do that," said Eisman.

Eisman and Dretke were anxious about driving across town should they get stopped by Hausa gangs. They covered the body and drove cautiously through town to the gravesite.

"It was a sight that I will never forget. Rectangular, big holes filled with bodies. Men, women, children, babies," said Eisman, who recalled seeing garbage trucks unloading with bodies.

They pulled the blanket off the man and removed him from the van, Eisman said. "We threw him in."

Chapter 9

Violence Winds Down

Several days after the atrocities had begun, Bill Cowley drove into Jos, witnessing the "desolation."

"You say something looks like a war zone. This was it. Bodies, corpses everywhere. Lots of blood," he said. "It was just human devastation."

The Igbos "were killed mostly with machetes and clubs…It was not a fancy operation. It was a brute force operation…The bodies were mangled. So, that's what you saw," said Cowley.

Brethren missionary Buzz Bowers said, "In the streets, we would see their bodies, face down, generally men. Pants had been removed and shoes. They would strip them of their pants and shoes as loot. Leave the body where they had struck them down. I was kind of shocked to see that."

Given the carnage, Bowers expressed initial disappointment that the Jos police didn't seem to have sought to quell the atrocities.

Sudan United Mission leader Geoffrey Dearsley offered a slightly different perspective. "As far as we can gather the Police were completely helpless in all this to do anything to prevent it, but whenever there was opportunity they seem to have helped…They were able to steer off the gangs from the railway station and seal off a group of Ibos there and they also set up an enclosure at the Police Station where any who escaped there were safe."

John Price recorded in his diary on September 30 that he went to school. "Parents saw 5 dead people on one street. Kids at school [had] many different stories."

"I myself saw bodies lying by the road throughout the town. I saw many houses that had been looted and many businesses that had been looted. On Friday morning in our own yard, a man was beaten to death. We thought that he was dead. Later, we revived him but they came back a second time and beat him again. The boys said he was beaten by Christian men," said Sudan United Mission leader Edgar Smith, a long-time and much respected Nigerian missionary.

Speaking at an ad-hoc meeting of missionary and Nigerian leaders a week after the disturbances ended, he continued sharing what he had witnessed. "I saw many carrying home the goods that they had stolen, and we identify many of them as being Christians living in this city."

Dearsley wrote that on September 30 a gang had come to their compound, but had not found an Igbo who had been hiding in the rocks in the back of the property. "We later managed to get police protection for him to be taken to the Police Station."

Dearsley witnessed, "From about mid-morning the Army and the Police worked together clearing the town of gangs and disarming them of their sticks and hatchets and bows and arrows. As they were driven out they worked their way through the suburbs and one man was badly beaten up on Ed Smith's compound and left in a ditch."

Dearsley and Smith took the man to the General Hospital, "where similar cases were coming in far quicker than they could possibly deal with."

Smith recalled that on Friday morning "about 10 o'clock, there was a sudden change. The Army disarmed the rabble-rousers and sent them home."

"I think we were told on the first day by our grape-vine friends that this would last four days…And so by Friday, it was over," Cowley said. "Shops were open…It was business as usual."

In Nigeria, people didn't have refrigerators, he said. They needed a fresh food supply every day, meaning the market had to open. And it was.

While the killings wound down, other problems intensified in Jos—disposing of the dead bodies littered across town, getting those hidden to safer locations, feeding the survivors who were clustered together, caring for those who had been injured, evacuating the Igbos. Each challenge had an immediacy to it.

Disposing of the dead presented a sanitary challenge in Jos. Bob Parham and Dave McCauley had already taken one body to the morgue.

"We were told that there were probably between 1,000 and 1,500 people that were killed on the Plateau. And that at one time there were 800 bodies in the morgue," recalled Jo Ann Parham.

Other bodies were taken to the mass gravesite. Eisman and Dretke had taken the Igbo killed in front of ELM House to that location. Many more corpses would be disposed of in the makeshift burial ground.

"The garbage trucks went through the town and picked up the bodies. Went to the Igbo section of town," said Wagner, noting that they were placed in a common grave.

"As I looked out, I wondered to myself, 'Why are the trash trucks out picking up trash now?' And it wasn't until our night watchman came and told us that the trash trucks were picking up the bodies...He had walked by the city dump and he had seen where they had bulldozed deep trenches. And these trash trucks that had picked up bodies backed up to these trenches and just opened up the back end and dumped the bodies in the pits," said Sudan United Mission missionary Dean Petersen.

He said their night watchman was Hausa and felt awful about what he had seen.

"I knew they had dug that new mass grave," said Glenis Petersen, who had seen the pit being dug. She remembered the trucks traveling on the road in front of their house and "seeing those dead people coming in on those lorries."

"It was a sad time to be there."

Jo Ann Parham recalled, "After these atrocities, the European community and the missionaries began to get together and think what can we help with this situation. How can we save lives? And so they thought if we can separate the Hausas of the North from the Igbos of the East, perhaps lives could be saved."

They obtained a small plane—either a Christian Reformed Church or Sudan Interior Mission plane—to transport four severely injured Igbos to the East. "Bob went with that first group," she said of the flight from Jos to Enugu.

Baptist missionaries meeting in Enugu met the flight. Parham's account was the first they had heard about what was happening in the North.

At the same time that missionaries and the European business community were devising a strategy of separation and evacuation, others faced the humanitarian challenge of feeding the survivors and caring for the injured Igbos who had gathered by the hundreds at the city's large police compound.

Chapter 10

Police Compound Becomes A Sanctuary for Fleeing Igbos

Edgar Smith recalled that on Thursday evening, September 29, he heard that Igbos were being cared for by the police. He then visited the police station, where he counted over 100 Igbos. "The following day at 10 a.m., there were no less than 14 lorries filled with people" at the compound.

Having observed that the police had not done much to quell the gangs, Buzz Bowers noted that they realized that the police had to do something to help the Igbos. "So, they made their station a hospital site, a refugee place, where the Igbos could come in."

Word spread throughout the community about the sanctuary of the police station and the need for immediate aid—medical attention, food and clothing.

Bill Cowley recalled that "a plea went out from the police that all these people. They had no supplies for them. They had no food. They had no clothing. They needed whatever help anybody could give. And people began to bring in supplies…Some of our mission houses and mission compounds began to send supplies down there to share with the people."

He announced late one afternoon to the high school that Igbos in the police compound needed clothing, thinking that "was best thing we could put together." The next morning, he found a "mini-mountain of clothing, used clothing just piled up there…Well, I knew the students. I knew their clothes. I saw some garments in that pile that they could not afford to be without." He took some of the donated clothes and gave them back to those students, while taking other clothes to the police compound.

Carl Eisman, too, heard about the needs at the police station. "We had obviously heard throughout the night that a lot of Igbos had been taken to the police compound. There was a need to care for them. We had also heard that it was a transit point, that it was temporary. And that the Igbos were going to be safely taken back to their homeland…We wanted to see if our Igbos were there, if they were okay, or if in fact, they had left already…and to see if there was anything we could do to help." He and Dretke headed there on Saturday, October 1.

"The police compound had a very tall mesh fence around it. I'm guessing 8 to 10 feet. Large compound. It's where they had all the vehicles, etc. It had two big gates that were secure," said Eisman. Armed police officers opened the gates and let them drive in.

"We saw, I would guess, more than 2,000 people, milling about…in shock, starving…We saw children walking around not knowing where their parents were. We saw parents walking around calling for their children. We saw one mother calling—wondering where her baby was. And her baby was swaddled on her back and the baby was dead. She kept walking, saying 'Where's my baby, where's my baby?' Very few men, but some."

Eisman said a "lot of people were in need of medical care. They had cuts, bruises, mostly around their arms and face where they had been beaten."

Buzz Bowers described the police compound as "fenced…good protection from attackers on the outside."

What he witnessed inside was "a lot of people on the ground, head bandages and other body parts bandaged. It wasn't a proper hospital by any means...When we would work on the patients we got on the ground with them. No beds."

"I was dealing with one young man with wounds on his leg. And I took off the old bandage. His blood spurted up on me. He was trying to apologize for his blood getting on me. I said, 'That's your blood. That doesn't hurt me. I'm sorry for you,'" as he put on a new bandage. Another man "had a bad head wound. I gave him the hat I was wearing. It was a soft hat. I thought that would help protect his wounds, his head."

High school student John Price wrote in his diary on October 1, "I spent whole day at police station helping Ebos. I have never seen so many people with such horrible wound."

"I will never see a thing like I saw today. I saw cuts right to the bone and skull, eyes, punctured hands and fingers just hanging and broken bones and dead people," he said.

Price described the police station as "pure chaos" with a lot of wounds. "They were vicious wounds like machete chops...I remember strong men with their muscles cut all the way to the bone, punctured eyeballs...They were really beat up."

The situation was grim. Too few doctors and nurses were tending to too many badly wounded Easterners.

"There was such a lack of medical help that the doctors would ask if you would take a suture and needle and sow somebody's hand back on...I couldn't do that stuff...So I tended to do more cleaning of wounds," remembered Price. "There was one guy that they had already treated. He had thick matted hair...They had already treated him...I kind of felt sorry for him and had bonded with him. He was someone I wanted to help because he was so beat up. I just remember looking at him closely and there were three wounds covered by the hair, serious cuts to the skull that hadn't been treated. I called the doctors back and they took care of him."

Price was also enlisted to carry off the dead, to separate them until they could be removed from the compound.

One of Price's classmates was Linda Scholten, who lived at Mountain View Hostel, the location for the children of Christian Reformed Church missionaries. Like other hostels, older Mountain View students were given the opportunity to go to the police station to meet the pressing needs of the surviving Igbos.

"Boy, I had the weekend of my life. I'll never forget it, I don't think… Saturday morning Uncle Dick, Kurt, Allen and Bill went down to the police station to see if the hostel could bring some food to the Ibos," she wrote on October 3 to her parents who lived in Mkar, the region of the Tiv tribe.

She shared that an Igbo came to the hostel that morning, was fed and then taken downtown.

When the first Mountain View group returned at noon from the police compound, they said "replacements were needed."

"I'm not kidding when I say that I did everything the doctors did, except stitch and give shots…I haven't seen anything so awful in my life…When I was there 3 men died and were taken away. It didn't affect me at all while I was there, because I was so busy helping. I held skin together while the doctors sewed it together," she wrote.

"We would wash wounds, give some sort of comfort measure and give them aspirin. Give them a drink…Try to make them comfortable," she recalled. "I remember one in particular was a man who had been hit by a machete…He had a deep gash in his mid-body area…I knelt down and I was trying to clean his wound with cutup bed sheets."

Another Hillcrest high school student, Carrie Robison, whose parents were with the Assemblies of God mission, said her house parents asked the older students if any would be willing to go to the police barracks "because there were so many Igbos flooding the place."

She and the other missionary kids, known as MKs, whose parents were working in the Eastern Region "felt compelled to go." The hostel van drove 10 or so students downtown.

"It was supposed to be a sanctuary for those who could actually get inside. Of course, getting from outside to inside was sometimes an insurmountable problem," she said. "I'm not sure that when I was there that the police barracks were organized enough to be called a real refugee camp. It was new. It was chaotic. It was the only place…in the area…that people were told they could come in and be protected from the mob," said Robison. "It was pretty much a free for all."

She said, "I remember seeing a lot of very, very, very wounded people. Wounded physically and emotionally and spiritually. I remember seeing fear… You could almost taste the fear…I remember crying. I remember screaming. And I remember hopelessness."

The Igbos were "pouring in" and the medical staff "was overwhelmed," said Robison.

"We were pretty much told to help, help with whatever you could. So, the wounded were there. They were lying on the ground. They were in great pain and agony. We spent a lot of time just trying to clean wounds so the medical personnel could stitch them up," Robison said, remembering the lack of pain medication.

At times, she would bandage up a wound and cry with the injured. At another time, she used tweezers "to pick maggots out of a face wound because the man had been so horribly butchered…He had been hiding in the big rock formations…So we were cleaning his wounds."

High school senior Ruth Keeney went with the Bowers and other Church of the Brethren students to the police station.

"We had buckets of water or some kind of antiseptic soap in them. I remember a nun handing that to me," said Keeney, who had some experience working in a dispensary in the bush with severe wounds like snakebites. "The maggots were somewhat gross to say the least. I wasn't repulsed by it all, I just wanted so much to help the people. There wasn't anything that was too awful to look at not to be able to do it. Even the odor. And it did smell. There was quite a stench."

The wounded Igbos Keeney treated asked her to pray for them. "There was always, always a thank you."

"These were high school kids at the makeshift rescue camp doing 'amazing' things—they were bandaging wounds, cooking stew, praying with the Igbos," recalled Hillcrest teacher Carl Eisman. "These kids should be in school. They were thrust into this upheaval, uprising. They rose to the occasion."

As Eisman prepared to leave the site to return to ELM House to retrieve some possessions for the hostel's Igbo staff, he noticed Igbo men outside the fence. "We look on each side of the gate and there are people, men, lying—I'm not sure how many there were, might have been 15—and they were just lying out there. It was hot. They had been injured to the point that they couldn't get in. And one might say, 'Why didn't somebody come out and get them in?'"

He identified two reasons for why those injured men had not been assisted. "Everybody was so busy with so many people that had so many needs that they just had their hands full. The other was that there were Hausa gangs not more than 20 yards away, sitting on some rocks and boulders with their machetes, with some clubs. You looked into their eyes and you knew they were waiting for the opportunity to go down and finish the job."

Eisman and Dretke found a stretcher. They left the security of the fence. They began carrying each man inside the compound for medical treatment.

"It may have been risky for us…But we couldn't leave them there. We didn't feel like we were in a lot of danger…You had to do it."

Later that day, when Eisman and Dretke returned from ELM House, they discovered a doctor covering with a blanket one of the men who they brought into the compound. He had died.

They took the body to the mass grave—the one they had already visited—with a sergeant escorting them.

"We backed up the van [at the grave site]. The garbage trucks were continuing to throw bodies in," said Eisman.

They communicated to one of the gravediggers that they had a body. "He said, 'No, no, no, no, no. Don't put him here'…We asked the sergeant to come out…He lifted his gun toward the gravedigger and said, 'You take the body.'"

Next to the grave pit, they saw a Nigerian man "propped up against a tree—obviously unconscious. As a matter of fact, we thought he was dead. We walked over to him wondering why he wasn't in the mass grave. We noticed a machete chop right through his skull down into his brain. And he had apparently been sitting there for a while because there were maggots crawling in and out of his brain," said Eisman.

"We asked the gravedigger, 'Why isn't this man not there [in the grave pit]?' He said, 'He is not dead yet. I'm not putting him in until he is dies.' What could we do? We left."

What else could the missionaries have done in that situation? What could they have done in the broader context of the widespread atrocities? They had never been briefed about what to do in the midst of genocide. They were utterly unprepared, perhaps disorganized without centralized leadership. They lacked political power. They were reacting to demanding needs, perhaps anxious about their own safety. They wanted to do the right thing in a humanitarian crisis.

Chapter 11

Sunday at the Police Compound

On Sunday afternoon, October 2, I accompanied my mother to the police compound to distribute food. I don't recall what food we took. I suspect that it was some kind of soup or stew. It might have been loaves of bread.

My mother, Jo Ann Parham, remembered, "Expatriates cooked food and took it to the police station. I don't remember what we cooked, but whatever we thought they would eat. And took clothes…Trying to help them survive."

She said, "I suspect that almost all Europeans and Americans helped with cooking…Nigerians helped us. Not all the Hausas were aggravated and mad at the Igbos."

A seventh-grade classmate who lived next door to us, Beth Williams, said she remembered cooking porridge at their house and taking it to the police barracks.

Another MK, Marilee De Groot, an eighth-grade student, recalled going to the police station with "vats" of food that had been prepared in the

Mountain View Hostel kitchen. She called it "acha." She said she spoon-fed some Igbos and did medical procedures.

At the police station that afternoon, two memories have stayed with me. First, I recall how densely packed it was. One could hardly move through the crowd of Igbos. Second, I remember overhearing a partial conversation between two Igbo men. One vowed revenge against the Hausas. The other cautioned him, citing a biblical verse: "Vengeance is mine, saith the Lord." He was urging the man to leave the punishment in God's hand.

Other MKs were also at the police compound that afternoon.

In her letter to her parents, Linda Scholten wrote, "Sunday we went down with food and I saw some of the men I had treated. They remembered me!"

Writing to her parents on October 5, Ruth Keeney shared what she did on that afternoon.

"Sunday we were down at the police barracks aiding the Ibos…I helped in three different things. First of all when we got there Becky [Weaver, daughter of the school principal] and I were sent with two big dishpans full of some type of Nigerian roll to hand out to women and children. We asked these policemen to come with us so that they could help control the people otherwise we would have been at a loss of what to do with everyone reaching for food. Anyway the police organized them into a line…it was sad to watch them all come crowding up for food. Then I helped hand out milk and water to just everyone."

After distributing food to the Igbos, Keeney went to the medical section of the makeshift refugee camp.

"I was washing faces, heads, hands, etc.," she wrote.

One recipient told her who he was and what happened. The gangs entered his house "and took everything. They robbed him of everything including 100 pounds [the Nigerian currency]. And he was all beaten up. I was working on his head—it was totally infected and where I touched it, it felt just like a balloon in that it was all pus-filled under the skin…big cuts were all over it… it was sad. And already it smelled of decay. Anyway after cleaning it as well as I could, I called the nurse and she and I put medicine on it and wrapped it all up in bandages."

A few days after her weekend work at the police station, Keeney returned.

"I was on my way to wash some wounds…And this individual called my name…I had interacted with him on a variety of occasions…So, he called my name. I couldn't tell exactly where he was because of the number of bloody clothes on that particular matted area. But I got down and then saw him. I noticed that he had wounds to be cleaned…and also had maggots," she said. "So, I asked the nun if I could just stay there and clean his out."

The nun agreed.

"And then he asked if I could be his daughter because everyone in his family had been killed, except his older daughter that he thought was my age. She had escaped and he was praying that she was still alive. But he said, 'Could you be my daughter?'" said Keeney, who consented. "He asked me if I would sing some hymns and quote scripture for him. And so I did."

She recited Psalm 23, said the Lord's Prayer and sang the Lord's Prayer to him. "Then he said to me, 'I'm going home my daughter.'"

The Igbo man then died.

The nun went with Keeney around the corner where she wept. The nun hugged her. After Keeney composed herself, she returned and washed more wounds.

Keeney said that she bottled up that experience. She did not share it with others for 29 years.

Graphic showing approximate locations of key missionary-community sites in Jos during "the disturbances" in 1966. Graphic by Jennifer Percy.

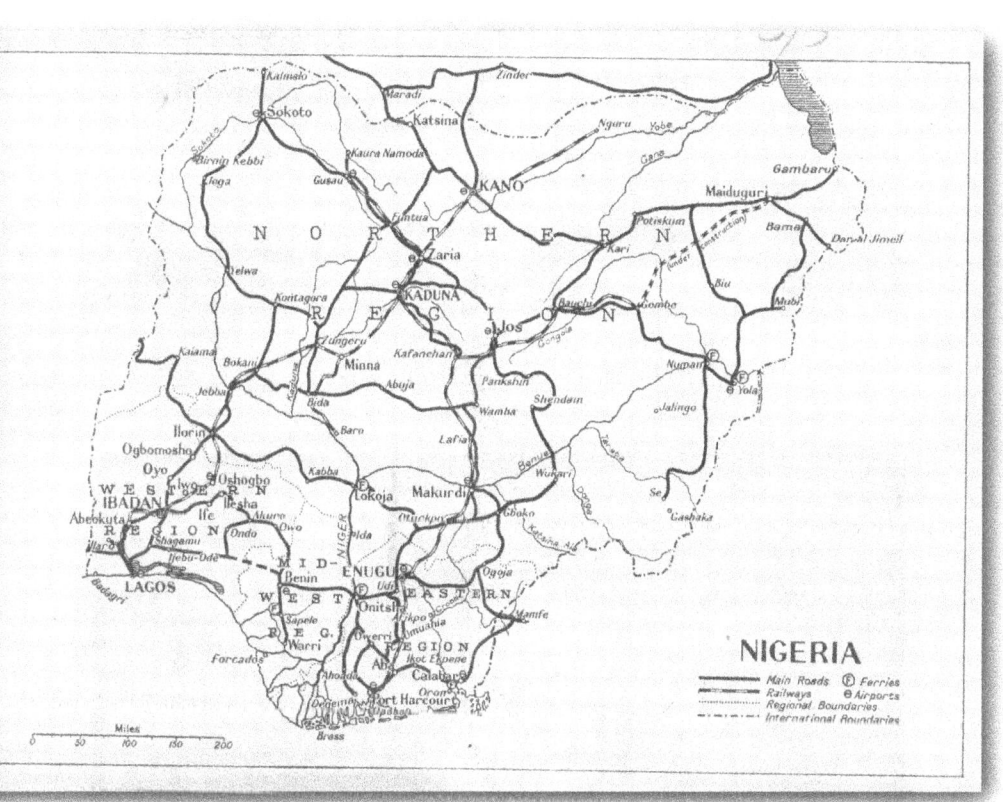

The 1966 map of Nigeria that was on the inside of the small diary kept by Sudan Interior Mission missionary kid John Price, Jr. Photo courtesy: John Price, Jr.

An aerial view of Hillcrest School in Jos in the 1960s. Photo courtesy: Phyllis Wagner.

The entrance to the Theological College of Northern Nigeria in Bukuru, near Jos. Photo courtesy: Harvey Kiekover.

The Disturbances

Baptist High School in Jos at about the time of "the disturbances" in 1966. The Cowley family is at center. To Bill Cowley's right sits Jonathan Ikerionwu, an Igbo student. Photo courtesy: Bill and Audrey Cowley.

Garba, the Cowleys' gardener, with the Cowley girls.
Photo courtesy: Bill and Audrey Cowley.

Timothy Olagbemiro (front row, directly behind trophy), a Yoruba student at Baptist High School in Jos. Photo courtesy: Bill and Audrey Cowley.

Phyllis Wagner, an Assemblies of God teacher at Hillcrest School. Photo courtesy: Phyllis Wagner.

Christian Reformed Church missionary Harvey Kiekover (far right) with Nigerian friends. Photo courtesy: Harvey Kiekover.

Lutheran Church-Missouri Synod missionary and Hillcrest teacher Beverly Knuth at the dye pits in Kano, Nigeria. Photo courtesy: Carl Eisman.

Longtime and well-connected missionaries
to Nigeria Nelle and Edgar Smith.
Photo courtesy: Alyce Peterson.

Paul and Margaret Griebel, missionaries with the Lutheran
Church-Missouri Synod. They are pictured here at
ELM House, the hostel for missionary kids from the
Lutheran Church. Photo courtesy: Carl Eisman.

The Makurdi Bridge, site of atrocities involving Igbos and Easterners being evacuated to the Eastern Region via train. Photo courtesy: Jon Low.

Ruth Keeney, walking at left, at her graduation from Hillcrest School in Jos. Paul Weaver, principal of Hillcrest, extends a hand of congratulations. Photo courtesy: Ruth Keeney Tryon.

The Disturbances

Dean Petersen and Glenis Petersen, missionaries with the Sudan United Mission. They offered aid during the Jos airlift. Photo courtesy: Archives of the Evangelical Lutheran Church in America.

The Bowers family from the Church of the Brethren mission: parents Buzz and Shirley, children Mark and Marla. Shirley kept shorthand notes of a critical missionary meeting in early October 1966. Photo courtesy: Brethren Historical Library and Archives.

Bob Parham and Jo Ann Parham, Southern Baptist missionaries. Bob Parham accompanied wounded Igbos on one of the first flights out of Jos back to the Eastern Region. Photo courtesy: Robert Parham.

Christian Reformed Church missionaries Helen and Herman Scholten, who helped evacuate Igbos and Easterners out of the Northern Region and into the Eastern Region. Photo courtesy: Herman and Helen Scholten.

The Disturbances

Karl Lundager, a Danish missionary and architect of many mission buildings, including the Theological College of Northern Nigeria in Bukuru. He is pictured here in the boulder formation at TCNN, where he would later find 26 dead bodies during "the disturbances." Photo courtesy: Karl and Bjorg Lundager.

The wounded at the Jos police compound. Photo courtesy: Marian Bricker.

Assemblies of God missionary kids Carrie Robison and Bobby Carlson help wounded people at the Jos police compound during "the disturbances" in 1966. Photo courtesy: Carrie Robison Young.

Giving aid at the Jos police compound. Standing in the center, in striped shirt, is Sudan Interior Mission missionary kid John Price, Jr. Just to his right, in striped dress and back to camera, is Christian Reformed Church missionary kid Linda Scholten. Photo courtesy: Marian Bricker.

The Opel Kadett Station Wagon belonging to Christian Reformed Church missionary Lee Baas, who used it to haul Igbos to safety in the Cameroons. Photo courtesy: Lee and Carolyn Baas.

Lutheran Church-Missouri Synod missionary Carl Eisman, on motorcycle, with fellow Hillcrest teacher and Church of the Brethren missionary Marian Bricker (foreground). Bricker took photos of aid at the Jos police compound. Photo courtesy: Carl Eisman.

A handwritten letter from Roger Ingold, field secretary in Nigeria for the Church of the Brethren, indicating the severity and danger of the crisis. Photo courtesy: Brethren Historical Library and Archives.

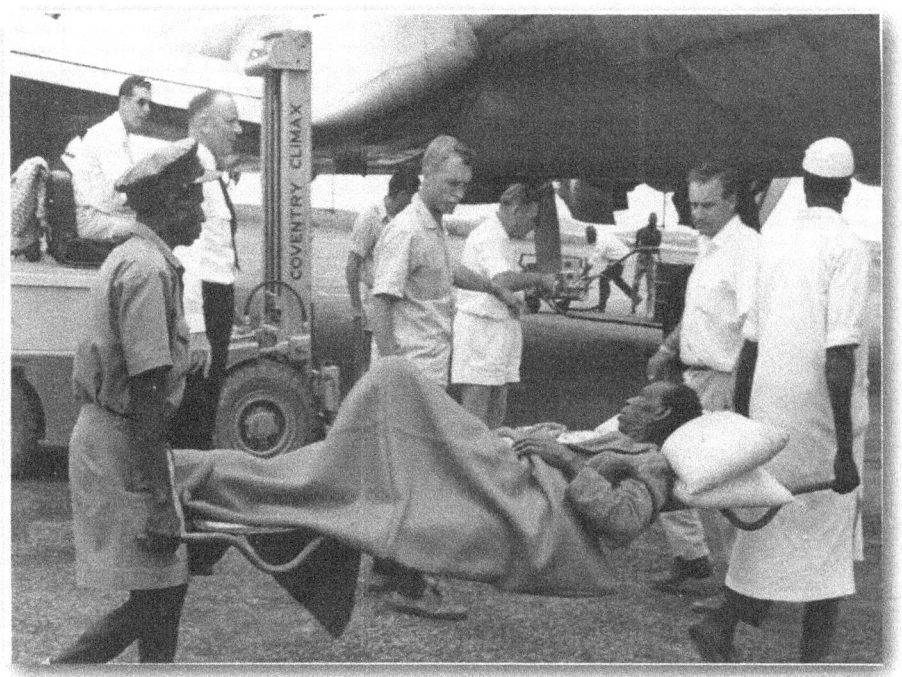

Bob Parham (center, with bandage above lip) joins other expatriates in helping evacuate wounded Igbos and Easterners from the Jos airport. Photo courtesy: SIM International Archives.

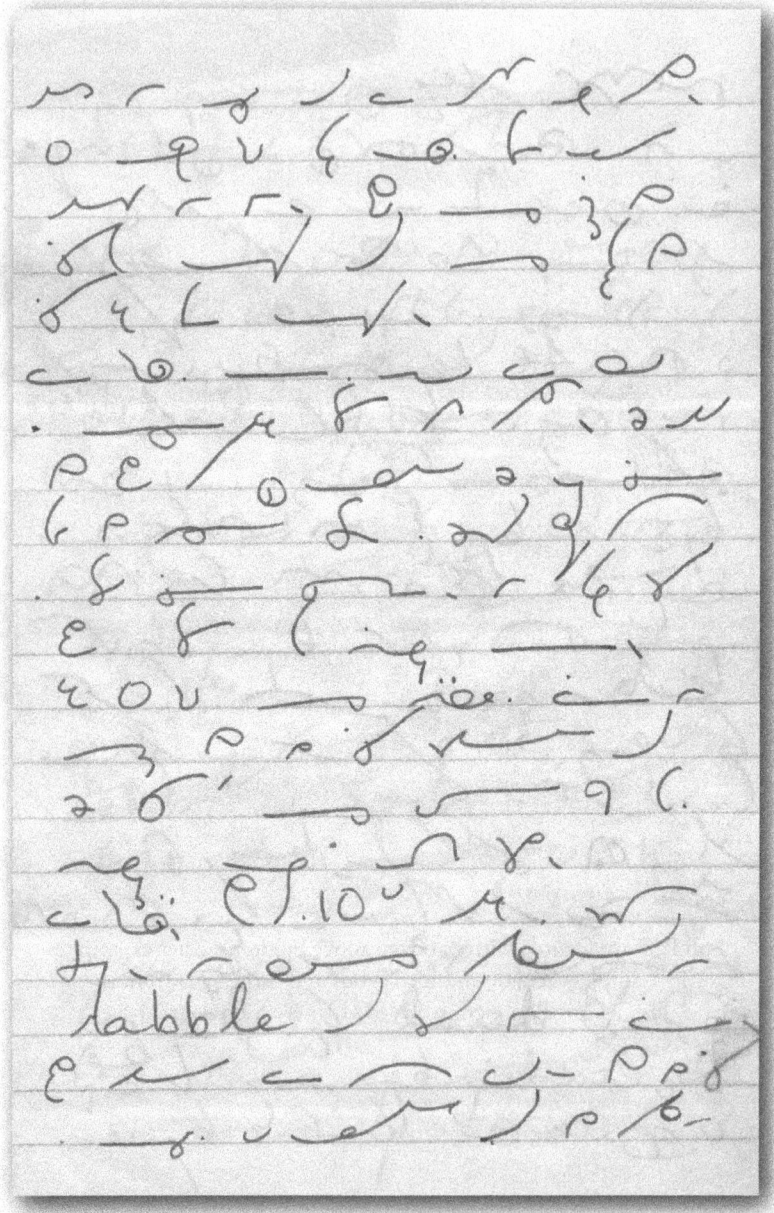

A page in shorthand from the notebook kept by Church of the Brethren missionary Shirley Bowers. Bowers filled more than 100 pages with shorthand during a private missionary meeting about "the disturbances" in early October. Photo courtesy: Buzz and Shirley Bowers.

The Disturbances

> Jos October 15, 1966
>
> Hello, Henry!
>
> I imagine you get bored to tears by form letters, but accept this one in lieu of a personal annual report! We are here in Jos with the other KBS staff for a week's holiday. The disturbances are over, for the present at least, and all has returned to quiet. We were even able to buy petrol all the way in, altho the stations may be living off northern reserves.
>
> The <u>big thing</u> that has impressed us over the last couple weeks is the great way in which our field secretary and the principal of Hillcrest both rose to the occasion under intense strain and proved themselves the leaders they are. After all emotions are quieted and dangers are past <u>do not fail</u> to get the inside story of the field secretary's role, not only with our own mission but with other missions and the Supreme Commander himself in this crisis and <u>also</u> get the inside story of the heroism of Hillcrest, from principal on down, including high schoolers, protection of human life in the face of personal danger. We are very proud of them and they themselves are <u>new people</u> as a result of it. The seriousness and tragedy of the crisis are exceeded only by the growth of these and others who have come through it. One of the minor servants,
>
> Chalmer

A letter from Church of the Brethren missionary Chalmer Faw to church missions executive J. Henry Long, in which Faw urges Long to get "the inside story" of what missionaries did during "the disturbances." Photo courtesy: Brethren Historical Library and Archives.

Yangkun Tuka, a Hausa pastor, and Jerry Falley, an Assemblies of God missionary, reunited years after Falley and other missionaries helped evacuate Tuka from Nigeria's Eastern Region. Photo courtesy: Jerry and Maxine Falley.

Bill Cowley, Jonathan Ikerionwu and Audrey Cowley are reunited at the Global Center at Beeson Divinity School at Samford University in Birmingham, Alabama, after more than 40 years. Photo courtesy: EthicsDaily.com.

Chapter 12

Mission to the Military Supreme Commander

Two missionary leaders decided to take a risky initiative—beyond hiding, feeding and caring for the Igbos. As Igbos poured into the Jos police station, dire reports from across the North filtered in. The humanitarian crisis was widespread.

They decided to ask the nation's supreme commander to intervene. They secured a small mission plane to fly them to Lagos.

"I'm on what may prove to be a dangerous mission—some will hate us for it and could seek revenge—it must be done," wrote Church of the Brethren field secretary Roger Ingold on October 1, in a hand-written airmail letter, to Henry Long, executive director of the Church of the Brethren mission board.

"Tomorrow another and I see personally the Supreme Commander to make an eye-witness report and request immediate relief for 2,000 refugees who could otherwise be completely eliminated."

Ingold, who lived in Jos and whose sons attended Hillcrest, said, "It has been terrible in Jos. Many Ibos and Southerners killed mostly clubbed and bludgeoned to death. Vast looting…We've hidden, fed, transported refugees to save lives. Medical services also given."

He wrote, "I may have to be replaced for coming here. I can do no other thing in clear conscience. The 2,000 are presently under police protection but it may be removed any time…We are here to tell what we know and to ask help."

Two weeks later in a letter to Henry Long, Ingold praised the Sudan Interior Mission for its support.

"SIM have given to me magnificent service in air travel whenever I have requested it," he wrote. When he and Edgar Smith went to SIM field director about their urgent mission to Lagos, "he gave us a plane and forty minutes later we were in the air."

Geoffrey Dearsley, a Sudan United Mission leader, wrote what he learned about that trip.

"In talking with Ed Smith during the day and in consultation with Roger Ingold, the SIM, Hillcrest folk, etc., it was thought that the Supreme Commander, Yakubu Gowon, would be completely unaware of our situation and the SIM agreed to fly down Ed and Roger Ingold to Lagos with the hope of obtaining a personal interview with him," he wrote in a nine-page letter to his home office in London on October 3.

"This is in fact what happened and they spent one and a half hours with him and our assumption that he was completely unaware of what was going on was true," said Dearsley. "He said he would make every effort to help with a train for the refugees."

Noting that a train had yet to arrive, Dearsley did say that on Sunday morning 23 lorries with 800 Igbos had left Jos.

Hillcrest high school student Bill Scholten wrote to his parents on October 3 about what he had heard about the meeting with Gowon from Edgar Smith, whom he referred to as "Uncle Ed."

Edgar Smith was not Scholten's biological uncle. Missionary children used the words uncle and aunt as terms of endearment for adult missionaries. It was a way to build a sense of family.

Smith had gone to Lagos on Saturday or Sunday to request a conference with Gowon, said Scholten, noting that Smith had an audience with Gowon.

"Uncle Ed said that they opened and closed with prayer. He said that Gowon agreed to do something for the Ibos…and it looks like he has," wrote Scholten.

On October 19, Ingold said in a letter to Long: "I was indeed deeply moved when two days later I saw the fruit of the effort [meeting with Gowon in Lagos]. I stood alongside the track and watched the heavily laden train move out with a great number of refugees."

Missionaries had a high view of Gowon, a Northerner, but not a Hausa. More importantly, he was a Christian. Gowon did not disappoint them.

Chapter 13

Jos Evacuation

Missionaries and the European business community determined that the best way to reduce future killings was to evacuate the surviving Igbos from Jos—immediately.

"I urgently request authorization to use up to $5,600, maybe more later, for emergency feeding and especially transportation of refugees. The transport is essential. 1. To remove them and to prevent future violence, chaos and warfare. 2. To literally save defenseless persons from being butchered!" Roger Ingold scribbled in a letter to Henry Long in early October.

"Literally thousands homeless without food, clothing and funds. Thousands of refugees—some thousands (3-4) have been removed by missions and commercials firms."

Audrey Cowley, too, appealed to her mission board for financial support.

On October 3, she wrote Cornell Goerner at the Southern Baptist Convention's Foreign Mission Board. "We are anxious to know if we as a mission can help financially in evacuation efforts…The most effective means seems to be by air lift. The need is urgent."

The Disturbances

Their appeals came as the Jos airlift got underway.

"We have had a terrible nightmare this past week and have seen much bloodshed. People by the hundreds have been slain in cold blood. Many of the survivors here are being flown out by special plane and some are leaving by escorted road convoy," wrote Dean Petersen on October 3 to his mission headquarters in Minneapolis.

Petersen said the Jos airlift began on Saturday, when Igbos were transported by lorries from downtown to the airport at the outskirts of town.

At least two different aircraft were used. The DC-6 had seats for 68 people; the Fokker Friendship 27 had seats for 28 passengers.

"That was quite an experience to see those people loaded on the plane. They would take as many as they could and put them in the baggage compartment towards the rear of the plane. And then we put the larger people in the seats and then smaller and if it was a child…There were sometimes two or three people deep on those seats. We had to make sure we didn't get it too overloaded," said Petersen.

The fastest way to load the planes was by forklift, he recalled. "It was to speed up as much as possible to get out as many refugees as we could to keep the planes moving," said Petersen.

Jo Ann Parham also remembered the forklift. "They came to the conclusion that they could take a table from the airport, cut off a couple of legs, put it on a forklift, tie it down, and lift the people up to put them in the airplane."

"These people were afraid and nervous, part of their family may have been killed and they had lost their possessions. Maybe they had saved a few things that would fill a pillow case…But they couldn't take that either because of the weight," said Parham. "They put one person in a seat. Another person sat in that person's lap and they could not take anything with them because they were afraid the plane would not lift up over the mountains nearby."

Neither Parham nor Petersen could recall the number of flights. But Petersen guessed that flights occurred every two or three hours and ran from Saturday until the following Friday. Flights went from Jos to Enugu or Lagos—and back again.

To keep the shuttle going, other missionaries prepared food for the pilots so they would not lose time going into town for meals.

Glenis Petersen's role in the airlift was to prepare food for pilots "so that they could get turned around." She baked cakes, made sandwiches, fixed salads—and even delivered cigarettes to the pilots.

"They've been evacuating by plane from here...Yesterday alone, they got rid of 750 by plane. Today, they took all of the sick out to the airport, put them on stretchers and fork-lifted them into planes," wrote Hillcrest high student Bill Scholten to his parents on October 3.

Writing in his diary, John Price recalled two plane loads of Igbos leaving on October 3. The planes were DC-6 aircraft.

Geoffrey Dearsley credited much of the Jos airlift to managers of private firms and banks. He noted that one day some 600 Igbos were flown south on a DC-6 and two Nigerian Airways Fokker Friendships.

He also wrote that in addition to the airlift, Igbos were packed onto lorries.

"Twenty-three lorries and about 800 people were being assembled and eventually got off the very early hours of Sunday morning," he wrote.

Bill Scholten shared with his parents: "Last night, the second convoy of trucks with Igbos left. It was really impressive to see those 14 pairs of headlights come laboring up the hill."

The surviving Igbos were traumatized, but not without gratitude, which they often expressed.

Jo Ann Parham recalled one such expression during the airlift.

"One time, while Bob was at the airport, a man called and said, 'Rev. Parham, you don't know me but I know you. And the Yoruba pastor in my church saved my life by hiding me,'" recalled Parham. "And he said he was grateful for what…the missionaries were doing to save their lives."

While expatriate business leaders and missionaries had initially planned to pay for the airlift, Roger Ingold told Henry Long on November 24 that the Northern Government "paid for all of the airlift operations including those from Jos and Maiduguri."

He wrote, "We did not need to pay a share of this."

Chapter 14

Outside Jos: More Atrocities, More Rescues

Massacres took place across Northern Nigeria. Reports of the involvement by the military and police differed sharply from city to city, town to town. Some were positive examples of intervention; others were examples of where officers instigated the killings. Often police and army seemed at odds.

Rescues of Igbos by both national pastors and missionaries were risky and widespread—and far more common than recognized.

Outside of Jos, in the small town of Barkin Ladi, "Yoruba pastor Rev. Akanji participated in the burial of fifty-nine Ibgos," wrote Jo Ann Parham in her memoirs.

Sudan Interior Mission leader William Crouch spoke of the mutiny of soldiers in Kano, where Igbos were killed inside the airport. Those who fled to the mission compound were shot. A large number of Igbos were killed at the railway station. Even missionaries themselves had narrow escapes.

"This went on all night and all the next day…There was a complete breakdown of government…The soldiers and hooligans were allowed to spend 24 hours in killing the Ibos in Kano. They estimated as high as 1,000 Ibos were killed in that period of time," said Crouch.

A pastor from Kaduna said the "hellions" started the killings. But the army quickly moved in trying to stop the killings. Nonetheless, Igbo homes were looted and an Igbo church was burned.

The abundant accounts of atrocities are not the full story of what happened in northern Nigeria, however. Remarkable stories of heroism also occurred.

One occurred in Kaduna. According to Baptist missionary Dewey Merritt, E. O. Akingbala, pastor of First Baptist Kaduna, a Yoruba congregation, disguised Igbos and drove them to safety.

Asked to explain what his father did, his son, John Olusola Akingbala, shared what he remembered.

A week before the attacks began, "there was fear and unrest in the Hausas in Kaduna promising revenge on the Igbos and asking for the country to be divided ('araba')," wrote Akingbala, who had been born in 1945 in Jos and is now a professor at Bowen University.

The following Friday, he had no more stepped off the front porch of his father's home than he encountered "a crowd wielding axes, cudgels and dangerous weapons." A few minutes later on the bus, "we ran into several wild mobs and corpses littering the road, slaughtered in unimaginable manners. We meandered through streets trying to avoid both mobs and corpses but several times this was impossible and we had to make U-turns to reach passable areas." The mob even stopped the bus to ask whether any of the passengers were Igbos.

When he finally arrived at his office, he called his parents about the safety of two Igbo women who lived with them. One was a teacher, Caroline; the other was a bank clerk, Miss Eke. On the first pass down their street, the mob had ignored the Akingbala house. However, the mob returned, asking for the Igbo residents. His parents said they were not there and invited the mob to look into the house. The mob thought the pastor's house was hallowed. They feared to enter and backed away.

After a sleepless night, "Dad started calling for help. The missionaries could not help because they were under surveillance too and their government had cautioned that they should be on standby. He called some military men from the congregation, but no one dared intervene due to the tension within the military hierarchy. So, together with mom, they decided to dress up the girls in Yoruba attire, moved the car to the backyard and the two girls had to climb into the back seat, and they were driven to the airport. They were stopped at several checkpoints on their way, but were allowed to pass, because he was a well-known pastor and an old one at that; really it was because the Lord was with them."

At the airport, with hundreds of Igbos waiting to be evacuated, the possibility of their two houseguests getting on board appeared unlikely. That was when Mrs. Akingbala took charge. She demanded that the two girls be able to get on a flight. She got her way. The girls got safely to the Eastern Region.

Years later, Caroline returned to teach in Kaduna. As for Miss Eke, they never heard from her again.

Another account of heroism came from acting field secretary for the Christian Reformed Church, Chuck Jansen, who lived in Mkar. He said the denomination had a number of Igbo teachers. Concerned for their safety, the missionaries hid them in hills and took them food before driving them to safety in the Eastern Region.

Jansen reported that in both Gboko and Markurdi "Ibos were rounded up. Some were shot, some escaped, and some were allowed to go free on lorries."

He added, "Christians in the area have been trying to extend their help to the Ibos in hiding."

Other Igbos were not nearly so fortunate.

Several missionaries recalled accounts of Igbo survivors who were on trains that were stopped and Igbo passengers were slain. Baptist missionary David Jester told of government officials informing him that a refugee train would take Igbos to the South and that their safety was guaranteed. He got some Igbos to board the train. Outside of Minna, the train was ambushed. The Igbo passengers were then murdered. Christian Reformed Church missionary Dirk Vander Steen said he heard about the halting of a train in Makurdi with the same results as in Minna.

Lee Baas witnessed what happened to one train at the Makurdi bridge as it crossed the Benue River. Makurdi was a central crossing point around an hour-and-a-half drive from Mkar and only a few hours from Enugu.

Igbos had traveled from Kano and other cities southward to safety on a federal government train. Perhaps this was the train that Supreme Commander Gowon had promised Roger Ingold and Edgar Smith after the Lagos meeting.

At the one-lane bridge, the train was stopped. The military and police stopped the train and shot all the passengers.

"I was there," said Baas. "There are few scenes that never leave you and that is one of them."

The Makurdi bridge atrocity underscored the tenuous nature of military leadership and the chaotic nature of the armed forces.

"I have the highest respect for General Gowon...He has always been a straight-shooter, upright...One of the great people of Nigeria," said Baas of the man who had gone to the mission school in Gindri, in the Tiv land, another place of heroic action to save Igbo lives.

Geoffrey Dearsley wrote the Sudan United Mission headquarters in London on October 3 that on Thursday and Friday "gangs threatened to come on to the compound for the Ibo students and 20 of them were hidden in various stores at Gindiri."

When the gang arrived on Friday, non-Ibgo students stood their ground, blocking the mob from attacking a man named Edet and his family, who were not Igbos, but Easterners.

Dearsley recalled that Maurice Cottom, principal of Boys' Secondary School in Gindiri, and missionary John Dean drove Edet, his family and Igbo students to the Jos police station.

"Mongu was known to be a very vulnerable point, but just as they reached there a terrific storm broke and they went through without incident," wrote Dearsley. The thunderstorm had covered up the sound of the lorry.

Mkar had one of the more unusual stories. The community had no Igbo population. It was a transit point southward, however.

When an influx of Igbos started arriving, they sought sanctuary at the Christian Reformed Church mission station. The missionaries hid them for a day or two until they had enough passengers to load a lorry to drive to Enugu.

The Disturbances

The driving assignment fell to Herman Scholten. Michiganders Herman and Helen Scholten had arrived in Nigeria only two years earlier. They went to Mkar for language study, arriving on Helen's birthday and a day of celebration—the day the Bible was first released in the Tiv language.

Scholten was a builder and the maintenance man for all the machinery on the CRC mission stations. He supplied provisions for the mission work, often going to Enugu for airplane fuel, food, and cash for the mission work. He was the natural choice for the task of transporting Igbos.

During the daylight hours, Scholten drove a big flatbed diesel truck across the back roads, really no more than two-track dirt paths to Enugu. He made as many as 15 trips with 40 or so passengers on each trip.

"One time I distinctly remember taking Helen with me. On our way back…there was a checkpoint. They refused to let me through. They stopped the truck and hauled me to the army headquarters and questioned me…They eventually took me back to the truck and said I could go," he said. "Helen sat there for hours wondering where I was."

Yet overall, "we had no problem transporting these people…The soldiers [in Mkar] welcomed them [the Igbos]. It was a wonderful fabric for us to witness our activities, a wonderful witness for the Christian Reformed Church in Nigeria."

"Igbos were very grateful. The back of the truck was not very pleasant, because there wasn't room to sit. You had to stand. But you got there and got there safely. That was the goal and that's the goal we accomplished."

Scholten said, "I've never talked publicly about what I did when I transferred people to Enugu…I didn't know if anyone was interested. I don't recall after all these years anyone ever asking me about the time." He never wrote his family in the U.S. about what he did. Never told his children about it.

Chuck Jansen reported that in both Gboko and Markurdi "Ibos were rounded up. Some were shot, some escaped, and some were allowed to go free on lorries." "Christians in the area have been trying to extend their help to the Ibos in hiding."

The Northern atrocities sent waves of anxiety through the Western Region, the tribal area for the Yorubas. Igbos there feared for their lives.

Baptist medical missionary Keith Edwards wrote in his diary on October 10 about a visit from Wallace Duval, the principal of the Newton Memorial School, a missionary boarding school sponsored by Southern Baptists in the Yoruba city of Oshogbo.

"Wallace Duval came over on Friday and said that all the Igbo cooks at the children's school had decided to go home to the East. This leaves the school without enough help to cater for the nearly one hundred children there. So he was looking for some catering help," wrote Edwards. "When the cooks at school announced that they were leaving everyone was most sympathetic. The school officials even offered to pay their transport home, and give them an extra month's pay so they could get a new start. Instead of seeming to appreciate this I hear that they demanded that the school promise to find them jobs in the East."

Edwards noted that two of their own employees had already left for the Eastern Region, as well as two hospital employees. One worked in the x-ray department. When he left, Edwards had trouble getting needed x-rays.

His diary entry on October 24 noted: "The latest rumor here is that Homer Brown called Dr. Ayorinde [a Nigerian Baptist leader] to say that it was strongly rumored in the North that the Hausas were going after the Yorubas on October twenty-ninth. Most rumors have been surprisingly accurate so far. Now we must wait five days to see if this one is true."

A month later, he wrote that the October 29 rumor was wrong.

The Northern atrocities sparked a backlash in the Eastern Region. While the overwhelming percentages of atrocities took place in northern Nigeria, reaction set in as the flood of Igbo refugees returned to the Eastern Region. Revenge killings started.

Assemblies of God missionary Jerry Falley recalled his first experience at seeing the returning Igbos in Enugu.

A Kansan, Falley grew up raising cattle. After college, he and his wife, Maxine, raised their mission budget. They entered Nigeria in October 1961 via freighter. Met by Dave and Lois McCauley in Port Harcourt, they were whisked away to a meal of African curry.

Five years into their mission tenure, they had settled in Enugu, the capital of the Eastern Region.

"Maxine and I…were living in Enugu in the fall of 1966. I had been sent by my wife on a to-do job down to the market to buy some vegetables. And I remember buying some vegetables and I heard this noise and a crowd gathering near the entrance. And so, I went to see what was happening," he said.

"A truck…had come. And it was filled with Igbos from the North that were fleeing because of the genocide that was taking place…And they had been stopped by the Northern soldiers at the border coming into the Eastern Region and been stripped of their clothing, any possessions they had were taken. And they were huddled under this canvas," Falley said.

"The driver got out of the truck and was explaining what had happened at the border to the crowd who had gathered there. He noticed this Hausa man walking freely there in the market. And he said, 'How can this man be walking around here in our market when our people are suffering like this?' So, the crowd kind of turned on this man. And he ran into this storefront" only later to be escorted away by the police.

Falley knew of what had happened during the May massacres. The market experience was the first he had heard about what was now happening in the North.

The next day, he saw at the police station Igbos who had come in by train. Most had bandages.

At the airport, he witnessed more injured, bandaged Igbos. "That was probably the most touching experience for me…That's when I realized for sure what was happening."

Falley said, "What touched me was the injustice of it."

The Assemblies of God had one Hausa employee at their press in Aba, about an hour-and-a-half drive south of Enugu. Missionaries Monroe Robison and Andy Hargrave managed the printing press.

"I was in charge of a bookstore…and was organizing a literature evangelism program. We also translated our Sunday school material into six of the Nigerian languages. And one of them was Hausa," said Falley, who hired Yangkun Tuka to translate English material into Hausa. He knew Yangkun's father, who had taught Falley Hausa.

Falley had later hired his son to do yard work in order for him to have fees to attend the secondary government school.

Falley mentored Yangkun, teaching him to tithe, read Scripture, how to witness.

With the influx of so many Igbos in the Eastern Region, they started forming Hausa gangs, he said. "They were out to kill every Hausa they could find. They were going door to door. They had been doing this for a couple of days in Aba. When it started, Yangkun stayed overnight at the press."

Falley told Yangkun to hide in the attic. After seeing bodies on the road, Falley drove Yangkun 150 miles to Enugu the next day. Driving up on a lorry on the one-lane road, a group of Igbos recognized that Yangkun was Hausa. They started yelling and tried to get the driver to stop. Falley accelerated around the truck.

Upon arrival in Enugu, Falley left Yangkun at the police station. The police placed him that night on a train heading north.

"We heard via missionaries that he had arrived safely...We didn't hear from Yangkun for 10 or 15 years," said Falley.

On a six-week mission trip back to Nigeria in the 1980s, "we stopped at the northern Bible school in Rahama...All of a sudden here came Yangkun... We hugged each other."

The Hausa man, who had been trapped in the Eastern Region and could have lost his life—Yangkun—had become a pastor.

Chapter 15

Smuggling Igbos Across Jos to the Airport

Having hidden Igbo faculty members and students, Bill and Audrey Cowley faced their next challenge—when and how to transport them to safety through roadblocks and across questionable roads once littered with corpses.

"Our plan is to keep them secure until we could find out what to do. There had to be some alternative coming up some day. And sure enough, our friends told us that there will be a plane coming through on such a day…at least a week after the killings had ceased…If you can get them there, they can get on the plane and get to safety," said Bill Cowley.

"We had to travel across the city…Things were still a shambles. Police and military roadblocks were set up all over the place…I knew we would have to pass through all those," said Cowley. He believed that if he could get those manning the roadblocks familiar with his vehicle it would be to his favor.

"So I drove through all of those points many times—all hours of day and night because I wanted at any point who ever might be on duty…that they

The Disturbances

would have seen me a couple or three times before and recognize the vehicle and recognize me in it. Having already inspected the vehicle two or three times, they would recognize that there was nothing in there to be concerned about," he said.

When word arrived early in the morning that they needed to head to the airport, Cowley loaded the Ibgos into the center of a VW van. They included students Jonathan Ikerionwu, Ebere Chukwu Emuwa, Ejeminhu Ahanotu, and Clement Nwachkwu, as well as two non-Igbo but Eastern faculty members—Mr. Wariboko and Mr. Madise.

He surrounded them with missionaries. The Cowleys placed their two girls in the back of the van on a ledge in order to obscure probing eyes looking into the van. He had the Igbos in Northern dress.

Cowley's plan worked. Officers waved him through the checkpoints.

When they arrived at the airport, they began the long wait.

Cowley described the day: "We waited, and waited, and waited. We tried to occupy ourselves. I remember Audrey took knitting along. And she knitted the world's longest scarf that day…It was a matter of milling around and talking to people, trying to encourage people, trying to say, 'Cheer up, things are getting better today. Today it's going to happen.'"

"It was the longest day of my life," he said. "I wondered when, when will it finish?!"

One of the Igbo students who had been hidden was Jonathan Ikerionwu, whose family had lived for many years in Bukuru. He was 17 years old. Before the late September genocide, his mother and all of his siblings left for the East. His elder brother and father remained at the Consolidated Tin Mining Company.

Ikerionwu recalled 50 years later that the Cowleys showed up at the mission house, instructed the hideaways to pack their belongings, and told them they were going to the airport.

The van ride to the airport "was an experience" that frightened him, he said.

The Baptist High School van went from the school to the airport. "More than six times, it went to the airport and came back…went back to the airport. So that all the security men and all the people around will see the people in the van were not Igbos."

Ikerionwu said the Cowleys "got some Yoruba students who had some tribal marks," some white children and other non-Igbo staff members in the van. Each designed to disguise the Igbo passengers. If the van was stopped at a roadblock and the guards saw men with Yoruba tribal markings, they were more likely to assume that the other Nigerian passengers were Yoruba.

On the trip across town, the Igbos laid "down in the van while the others were sitting up. So that nobody would see us. Miraculously, when the van was taking us to the airport…nobody stopped us, nobody stopped the van to find out who was in the van," Ikerionwu explained.

He said that when they arrived safely at the airport, everybody said, "Thank God."

Yet the anxiety wasn't over. They spent hours at the airport waiting for the plane that would take them to Lagos.

"When we were at the airport, I think it was a Nigerian Airways that was to have flown to Jos to fly back to Lagos. But that plane did not come. I don't know why it didn't come. I suspect that at that time, most of the workers in the airports were Igbos. And most of them left. And because of that, it was not possible for planes to land or take off," explained Ikerionwu about the long, nervous wait for a plane.

Word finally came of an arriving plane. But there was a problem. Night was falling. No one knew how to work the runaway lights. The airport staff had been Igbos. They were no longer there.

The pilot told the missionaries to line the runway with their car lights. They did so. The plane landed and took out on a runway lit by car lights, said Ikerionwu.

Back at the Baptist High School, the students still did not know what had happened to their classmates and teachers.

Yoruba student Timothy Olgabemiro said that the day after the flight had left Jos students heard what had happened. When they were told, "We were so glad that the Lord had saved them from being lynched," he said.

The Easterners were not safe on campus "because we were living in a Hausa village in Naraguta…They were nice to us," Olgabemiro said of the villagers. Despite the relationship between the villagers and the school community, which included the students shopping in the village market and the chief knowing well Bill Cowley, the villagers would have attacked the Easterners on campus.

The Baptist High School community was grateful that the Easterners were heading to the East. "We prayed for them at the school," he said.

Chapter 16

Rescue of Hycenth Adibenma

Working in the offices of Hillcrest School was a beloved Igbo named Hycenth Adibenma.

When the killings began, principal Paul Weaver hid him on campus—where was never clearly known. Faculty members and students had competing theories. Everyone, however, was in agreement that Weaver would later get him safely transported to the East.

High school student Bryan Hargrave wrote his parents at the Assemblies of God printing press in Aba on Tuesday, October 4. He explained that the post office and electric and water works in Jos were down to skeletal crews, since most of the employees had been Igbos.

"A lot of stores downtown were looted, and everything was taken, including the shelves," he wrote, "Pretty bad eh?"

He ran through the death tolls in the hundreds in Jos, Maiduguri and Kano. He recalled that an Igbo had been beaten in front of Miss Wagner's home. He wrote about the thousands of refugees at the Jos police station.

Then, he begged his father to help Adibenma.

"Dad, I want you to do me a favor. There is an Ibo coming down from Jos (probably already there) named Hycenth that worked here at Hillcrest as secretary. He is a very hard worker, dad, and he needs help desperately. All his money, etc, was taken away from him. Please dad, help him if you can. He was a very good friend of mine. A tremendous guy. But, there he is, without anything now. Dad, please if you can help him. If you can give him a job or if you can get him a job somewhere else. He is a very hard worker," pleaded Hargrave.

Adibenma did make it safely out of Jos.

He wrote Ruth Keeney on November 27 from Port Harcourt: "How are you doing? Also how is Hillcrest School and its daily activities?"

Adibenma shared that he had received a letter from Paul Weaver, who said Keeney was helping out in the school offices in the afternoons.

"Please, thank you for that while I regret any inconvenience that might cause you. I am sorry to have left Hillcrest, but I am grateful to God that I was free and safe over the 28/9/66 event, though many of my things were looted," he wrote. "Thank you once again for helping Mr. Weaver in the office work. Good luck to you."

Adibenma was safe, grateful, concerned for the community of Hillcrest.

The letter to Keeney seems to have been his final communication with the school. She never heard from him again. Neither did others.

Chapter 17

Jos Notebook: What Is Genocide?

Missionary leaders and Nigerian pastors met in Jos on October 7-8 to understand what had happened across the North to Igbos and other Easterners. They told what they had witnessed. They listened to reports from others. They questioned the dubious accounts attributed to secondhand witnesses, seeking to dispel rumors. They wanted the facts. They hoped that with a better grasp of those horrible days, they could prevent a recurrence.

Brethren missionary Shirley Bowers took shorthand notes at an ad hoc meeting.

"After we say what happened, we should then say what we think caused these things and what we can do about keeping it from happening again in the future," said long-time Nigerian missionary Edgar Smith.

Members then began sharing what they had witnessed, what they had heard from reliable sources, and what they had done.

The Disturbances

Their language was instructive. They used a variety of words to describe the perpetrators of violence. A frequent one was "hooligans." Others were "mobs," "rabble rousers" and "ruffians."

Knowing how to describe the widespread atrocities challenged the group.

Two Sudan United Mission missionaries—Geoffrey Dearsley and Cecil Webber—called the events "the trouble."

When Christian Reformed Church acting field secretary Chuck Jansen gave his report on what had happened in the Benue province, he referred to the events as "disturbances."

Nigerian pastor Ngamariju Mamza labeled the killings as "the disturbances" and "disturbance." Another Nigerian pastor, unnamed in the notebook, used the word "disturbance."

Telling of a conversation with a village chief, Ernst Højvig, a Danish missionary with Sudan United Mission, spoke of "the disturbances."

Nigerian Gin Maigari, chairman of the Evangelical Church of West Africa, also used the term "the disturbances."

"Disturbances" was the most frequently used word in the meeting.

Not once in their meeting did they use the word "genocide."

Perhaps they only associated genocide with the state-sponsored violence of the Nazi holocaust. Or perhaps they were uncertain about the death toll and lacked the confidence to say definitively that it was planned and executed. Or maybe they wanted to use a softer term to avoid inflaming an already burning environment.

Regardless, the events qualified as genocide, according to the already adopted United Nations definition of genocide.

The United Nations defined genocide in 1948 as "any of the following acts committed with intent to destroy, in whole or in part, a national, ethnical, racial or religious group, as such: killing members of the group; causing serious bodily or mental harm to members of the group; deliberately inflicting on the group conditions of life calculated to bring about its physical destruction in whole or in part."

A key component to genocide is the targeting of a group of people because of who they are or what they believe. Genocide is never a random act resulting in death. Genocide is organized, planned, and executed against one targeted group by another group, be it on racial or religious or tribal grounds.

The ugly word "genocide" comes from the combination of the Greek word for race or tribe, "geno," with the Latin word for killing, "cide."

Historian Godfrey Uzoigwe, an Igbo, who taught at both the University of Michigan and Mississippi State University, labeled what happened as genocide.

"It is very, very difficult to define genocide," said Uzoigwe. "The standard definition of genocide is that you have to be targeted because of what you are, because of what you believe. And that does not mean that if you are an Igbo or Hausa or Yoruba, you have to be killed for the crime to be seen as genocidal. But that you are targeted is important."

The holocaust is the most studied genocide in history, he observed. The Rwanda genocide was much more recent and easier to comprehend "than the

Igbo genocide." The events in Nigeria occurred when the communication system was rudimentary.

"The Igbo people have not made the kind of considered effort that the Jews or Armenians or Rwandans have done to make their case," said Uzoigwe. The Nigerian genocide "went under the radar" and "it was forgotten."

A genocide scholar himself, he acknowledged another issue when defining genocide. "There is the issue of numbers. But the numbers…must be substantially enough to cause a trauma. If you kill one or two people or 10 people who belong to a particular group, it will not have the same impact as if you kill a thousand or 5,000…or a million people or more," he said. "The number…has to be substantially large, systematic, and proven that those who were killed were targeted because of their ethnicity, race, religion or whatever."

He pointed out, "If you look at the Igbo genocide in the North, the figures range from 5,000 to 30,000 to 100,000 people killed. If you look at the population of the Igbos in the North at that time, the numbers are quite substantial. But nobody actually knows…Nobody also doubts that thousands of people were killed in appalling circumstances."

Another issue when defining genocide is planning.

Genocide "is not spontaneous…It is a series of choices. Genocides are planned, manipulated by a group of individuals who have interests to protect and they use the masses by appealing to their seamier side, the dark side of individuals," he said. "If you look at the Nigerian genocide, it was May 29, July 29, September 29…now what is spontaneous about that?"

He pointed out, "The killings that were going on in Jos, were going on in Kaduna. They were going on in the Benue provinces, in the Tiv country, and Sokoto, and Maiduguri, almost at the same time. That could not possibly be spontaneous. Somebody planned it."

This was "planned, organized, executed," said Uzoigwe. "Many of the individuals who are committing the act didn't even know the reason for doing it except something their leaders tell them. And the leaders go unpunished because it is difficult to find out who they are. Even if you know who they are you find it difficult to convict them in a court of law."

Chapter 18

Conflict Was Tribal, Not Religious

The Jos meeting voiced the strong opinion. Participants concluded that the killings were tribal, not religious.

"What they did here was purely a civil matter, and not something against religion," said Bitrus Pam, a Nigerian Church of the Brethren pastor.

"There is no evidence to indicate that there is religious importance here. I am very sorry to say this, but I think there are some of us who are trying to slant the whole thing so it would look as if this thing had a religious bias," said Pam, according to Shirley Bowers' shorthand minutes of the meeting.

Sudan United Mission leader Edgar Smith reported, "The boys said he was beaten by Christian men. Also, I saw many carry home the goods that they had stolen, and we identify many of them as being Christians living in this city."

Nigerian pastor Damina said, "As has already been stated, you cannot blame only the Hausa for this but some natives of different localities and even some Christians."

Another Nigerian pastor, Gin Maigari, underscored the involvement of northern Christians. "We were not happy because some church members had taken part in this."

Christian involvement in the killings and the looting reinforced the belief that the driving force behind the atrocities was tribal. It was not Muslims targeting Christians.

The belief that the conflict was religious gained momentum during the subsequent Biafran War, when Eastern leaders sought support from the West, especially the United States and United Kingdom.

Fifty years later, one is tempted to see the Nigerian genocide as religious, that is Muslims targeting Christians. To do so is to impose Nigeria's current problems of Muslim extremists onto the past. Neither Nigerians nor most Christian missionaries saw the 1966 atrocities as a religious conflict.

"The tribal allegiances far outweighed the allegiance to Christianity," said Lutheran missionary Carl Eisman. "Now whether one wants to admit that or not, there's quite a different thing. There are too many occasions that took place where solid quote Christians—Nigerians—harmed and/or murdered other people."

Eisman recalled a story where Igbo Christians killed Hausas.

He cautioned that one could not over-generalize about Nigerian Christians—and say that all converted Christians would allow their tribalism to outweigh their faith.

"The problem between these two tribes was not religious. While we were there in Nigeria, Muslims and Christians got along beautifully. There was no problem between the two religious groups," said Baptist missionary Audrey Cowley. "But the problem that came was the problem between Igbos and Hausas. There may be a bit of economics."

Assemblies of God missionary Phyllis Wagner underscored the Hausa resentment against the Igbos going back decades. She, too, acknowledged that economics played a role.

"Yes, indeed it was economic issues that influenced the difficulties between the Hausas and the Igbos," said Wagner. "This difficulty was tribal... Those atrocities in 1966 were tribal. Very different situation" than today.

"I would say it's not exclusively tribal, but with other connections. There was a real concern that the Igbo were the trade people. That Igbos were getting the good jobs...Igbos were the ones who were trained. They were the educated people. They were there who could do the job. They did the job. They were taking the jobs. They were there starting businesses in the towns," said Christian Reformed Church missionary Lee Baas.

He noted that "there was always a little hostility like there is between many other tribes," such as when the Fulani took their cattle into Tiv country and destroyed their fields. "But it ended up as almost a Hausa-Igbo conflict."

Baas especially recognized the historic role of education, pointing out that education and medical facilities were not that well received in the North like they were in the West, East and Middle Belt. So, things did lag, observed Baas. "It wasn't the fault of missionaries."

Having noted the role of education, economics and politics, he said: "I would be hard pressed to push it into a religious component."

He said, "There would not have been the Biafran War" in 1967-1970, when an estimated 1.5 million Igbos starved to death, without the atrocities of 1966.

Baas' fellow CRC missionary, Harvey Kiekover, said, "Everything was very tribal. The Tiv were separate. The Hausas were separate. They had their own languages."

He said, "Tiv and Hausa were totally different languages…Hausa was a trade language and Tiv was a local language."

"Everything there was so tribal. The Tiv against the Jukun and the Jukun [against the Tiv]…Tribalism was rampant," said CRC missionary Herman Scholten. "We did everything we could to not be tribal."

Helen Scholten shared that "It was during this time that the Tiv people would mark their babies, their men, their children with skin markings…This was a tribal sign." The markings were used to guard the Tiv from being mistaken as Igbo.

Hillcrest senior Ruth Keeney explained that Hausas and Igbos were afraid of each other, that one tribe would gain political power over the other. She saw education and economics as shaping the fear behind the conflict. Educated and trained Igbos were brought North to take over commerce, banking, business, causing jealousy among the Hausas.

"This was not religious. It was not Muslim-Christian. It was tribal," said SUM missionary Dean Petersen. "Igbos controlled practically everything…Education came to them first. And they naturally migrated North where their talents and skills were needed. And eventually, they took over the managerial positions."

The Northerners did not have the same advantages," said Petersen. "It was economic first because of the Igbos' controlling interests."

"What caused the troubles in African nations was not a religious thing as much as tribal, the hatred of tribe to tribe. We know that tribes used to have tribal marks on their face…to identify their tribe…People would kill because of what tribe you belong to. It wasn't religion so much," said Brethren missionary Buzz Bowers.

Nigerian historian Godfrey Uzoigwe added another explanation for the atrocities. He said that the loss of power was a driving force, noting that when the first coup of 1966 took place many people lost their power.

If religion played a role in the genocide, "it must be indirect…Religion wasn't the major issue…I think it was more economic and political…They had lost power and wanted to regain power…And they blamed the Igbo people for causing them to lose power," he said.

Uzoigwe thought that the Northerners were fearful that the Igbos would seek revenge and rise to power again.

To stop that from happening, the northern elite felt that "the best thing they could do was to drive them out of northern Nigeria. Let them go back to the East where they belonged," he concluded. "The northern elite would not be happy until the Igbos were driven out of Nigeria."

Another Nigerian, Timothy Olagbemiro, former chancellor of Bowen University, explained the social complexity of the conflict.

He said his Yoruba family had both Christian and Muslim members, as did many Yoruba families. That dynamic made it easier for Yorubas and Hausas to live side by side without conflict.

To illustrate this connectivity, he said that in Jos there was a mosque next to the Yoruba Baptist Church.

"When I was a kid, we used to play soccer inside the mosque," he said with a chuckle. "We just played together with the Muslim boys."

Moreover, "at Christmas time, we actually did Christmas together. When [there was a] Muslim festival, we ate together," he said.

The intertwining of two different faith groups—Christians and Muslims—among Yoruba families made it easier for Yorubas and Hausas to get along.

Such was not the case for the Igbos. They tended to remain separate. "Very, very few of them were Muslims at that time," observed Olgbemiro. Most of the Igbos were Christians, which meant that Christian Yorubas and Igbos got along well.

"Yorubas and Igbos were friends. Yorubas and Hausas are friends. But the Hausas and the Igbos were not too close because there was no forum for them, except master-servant relationship," he said.

The January 1966 coup was intended to deal with corrupt civilians. But no significant Igbos were killed, while major Hausa leaders were. This caused Hausas to fear the Igbos, fear that they were seeking power.

Fifty years after the atrocities, Olagemiro lamented that it could happen again.

"What happened in 1966 can still happen at any time. There is deep distrust between these tribes [Hausas, Igbos and Yorubas]. No trust at all. Any time it can fall into just a mess because of greed for power. Each group is just looking for that power to be leader," he said. "There is a lot of mistrust in Nigeria in a nation that has no fear of God. A lot of corruption in the country. Money is being made and people are stealing and stealing and stealing."

The thirst for money and power "is the problem," said Olagemiro, who contrasted such yearning with "a life of sacrifice" based on having "the mind of Christ."

From Olagbemiro's perspective, tribalism was a major force in the genocide coupled with the thirst for power and money.

Chapter 19

It Was Planned, But Who Planned It?

Genocide is never a random act resulting in widespread killing. Genocide is organized, planned and executed against one targeted group by another group for racial, religious or tribal reasons.

Baptist missionary Jo Ann Parham believed the killings were planned. Her proof was what happened in her own neighborhood.

"There was a search for Igbos carried out on the street over from ours. A gang went into different homes looking for their perceived enemies. Shower curtains were yanked back. Ceiling boards were punched open with long handled brooms or sticks. They were looking for anyone in the attic. Locked doors were rammed open. Every Igbo discovered was killed," she wrote.

Parham said, "We anxiously waited for them to march down Dan Dauro Road. Amazingly, they avoided the few blocks where we lived. Then we realized that not a single Igbo lived or worked on that street...[T]he people hunters had done their research. They knew where Igbos lived and worked."

The street on which we lived included two homes of Baptist missionaries and three homes of Islamic judges.

She was not alone in her assessment that the atrocities were planned.

"I think genocide does require preparation," said Audrey Cowley, another Baptist missionary in Jos, reflecting on what had happened.

Her husband, Bill, said, "Before that, it requires teaching…So, who knows when did a given genocide begin? When did grandparents, great-grandparents, ancestors begin to think such things and extend those to their children and grandchildren? And it continues to develop and snowball…until one day it breaks loose. So, I think it's a long process of teaching. We teach people to hate. We teach people to love."

He did think the Nigerian slaughter was coordinated. "It had to have been. I don't think we can lay it to mere coincidence that all these things of a very similar nature happened in a very similar way…almost at the same time. And those little details such as…we were told a specific day this would finish."

Cowley was unsure about who planned the massacres. "There had to be somebody back there where the buck stops."

"As I recall, it started up in Kano with the leaders up there. And then, I guess the leaders in Jos wanted to compete with the leaders in Kano," speculated Audrey Cowley.

The question of planning was discussed at length during the meeting of missionary and Nigerian leaders in Jos on October 7-8.

"We seem to agree that surely this seems to have been organized," concluded Sudan United Mission leader Edgar Smith. "To me it seems as if it was planned."

The chairman of the Evangelical Church of West Africa, Gin Maigari, a Nigerian, responded, "Rumors helped bring about these disturbances…It is very true that there has been a plan."

Chuck Jansen, acting field secretary for the Christian Reformed Church, shared a similar assessment. He said, "The rumors were not the actual cause. There had been a definite plan, and the rumors were just fuel."

Smith weighed in again: "In some places, it seems that it was the Army that did it. In other places, where there was no Army, it began involuntarily. This still means that there was a plan."

Danish SUM missionary Ernst Højvig observed that a "team" was behind the violence.

As the meeting drew to a close on the first day due to a curfew, Smith pressed the issue of the source of authority behind the plan. He suggested that the group take up that question the next day.

He asked, "Where did the plan come from?"

Højvig sharpened that question with another one: "Who could benefit from these disturbances?"

On a certain morning, Smith said that the hooligans started the killing and then immediately stopped. "They did not start until they got permission. Is that right?"

He noted that both the army and police acted to stop the killings. "They must get an order from somewhere."

As for village chiefs, they claimed that they lacked the authority to stop the atrocities. "But when it is wished to stop it, then you hear their voices."

Smith, who had met with Supreme Commander Gowon a week earlier in Lagos, said, "I say the authority does not come from the Supreme Commander…I felt convinced…that he really did not know what was going on in Jos. Now I propose that the Northern Military Governor does have authority in this matter."

Nigerian pastor Damina questioned Smith's proposition about the northern governor: "It is difficult to have any evidence to prove this."

Ngamariju Mamza, another Nigerian pastor, expressed the desire for proof before drawing conclusions.

"If we say people have permission, is there anyone who can say for sure he has seen the permission?" he asked. "Before we make some remarks, we must be sure it is true and it is real…We should not agree without real proof."

An unidentified person in the shorthand notebook seemed to want to blame the "hooligans." He observed that Northerners thought "Ibos should be repatriated from the North. If they left, the Northerners would have jobs. As a result, many people joined in the looting and killing."

After a number of stories were shared, Bitrus Sawa advised, "It is essential that we listen to both sides of the story if we are to make any decisions at all."

Church of the Brethren field secretary Roger Ingold returned to the question of the purpose for the killings. "What do you think is the one probable and the single purpose?"

Sawa, who would become the first Nigerian principal of Theological College of Northern Nigeria in 1968, said, "I thought that if there had been a plan in the North for what had happened, this would explain how everything happened at the same time."

As for Ingold's question about the purpose of the atrocities, Sawa said, "It was sheer retaliation."

As the day of the meeting wore on, the discussion turned to the role of Christians in genocide and the role of the church in the state—and then to the role of missionaries.

"We know that Christians were involved in this," said Smith. "How do we advise each other as to repentance for all of us including ourselves?"

In the next breath, he sought advice for expatriates "to our actions in the future. Some of these things are very terrible to us. We were not born here; we do not know as much as you know what we should do. What for the sake of Jesus Christ should we do in the future?"

The church should not "investigate the matters of the government. The government secrets cannot be disclosed to the general public…The government is not the church. They will kill as they wish. Our greatest concern here is that when there are disturbances what Christians should do about it," said Sawa.

The Nigerian pastor added, "We can't just protest and say we have nothing to do with this."

Gin Maigari agreed with Sawa that their task was not to investigate the government.

"But we have come here to look at matters that have affected the church for some Christians have taken part in these disturbances. Some people were involved to the extent that they even took part in beating and looting…Now what do we do?"

Regrettably, the second volume of the notebook in shorthand was lost. How the group answered Sawa's question is unknown.

In a memo after the meeting, Baptist missionary Homer Brown summarized what he heard: "It was felt by many…that the disturbances were planned. In support of their belief, they stated that: (1) The disturbances occurred at the same time throughout the North. The dates May 29th, July 29th, and Sept. 29th seem to be significant and support the idea that there was a plan behind all of the disturbances; (2) Many people knew the time the trouble would begin before it ever began; (3) The disturbances took place simultaneously throughout the entire North. It was believed by some that the plan had been in hand for a long time and that there was a power structure and an authority behind the plan."

Chapter 20

Shock and Silence Set In

Bob and Jo Ann Parham drove through the Igbo quarters after the genocide had ended in Jos.

"It was a wasted neighborhood...Windows and doors had been splintered into bits. Many doors had been ripped from the walls. One was torn ajar. It hung awkwardly on a single hinge. Not a house had escaped the destructive wrath," wrote Jo Ann Parham, 50 years later after witnessing it.

"In their rage, looters ripped out electrical fixtures. Not a stick of furniture was left in abandoned homes. The only car in the area was stripped of its tires," she said. "It is difficult to imagine how men busy at their jobs one day could go on such a berserk rampage the next to wreck and annihilate."

While some missionary and Nigerian leaders had faced in the October 7-8 meeting the difficult task of explaining how such an event could happen, most other missionaries and missionary children did little to process the disturbances in group-discussions.

A veil of silence fell after the Igbos had been evacuated from the North. When time came for reflection on the unimaginable and incomprehensible atrocities, missionaries kept quiet. They rarely spoke about the carnage among themselves. They almost never discussed it with their children. Over and over again, missionaries shared that they had not spoken publicly about what happened for 50 years.

The story was untold, maybe suppressed. But it was never forgotten, even bringing tears to those who recalled the traumatic experiences five decades later.

Jo Ann Parham did not know until 2016 what fellow Baptist missionaries Bill and Audrey Cowley had done in 1966. The Cowleys didn't know what my father did during the Jos airlift. Maybe the years erased the memories, maybe not.

Those who prayed and studied the Bible together—and labored in common fields—kept their own counsel. They guarded their experiences.

Some of their silence was encouraged. Some of their silence was personal choice.

Roger Ingold wrote Church of the Brethren executive Henry Long on November 24 about "a short but intense conversation" with the Northern Military Governor, who assured him of religious freedom.

"He strongly warned we missionaries to keep our 'tongues' out of the matter," said Ingold.

In a memo recalling the October 7-8 Jos meeting of Christian leaders "to consider the disturbances," Baptist Homer Brown wrote that he and Rev. Adamu had attended as the Baptist representatives.

Brown said that some in the group felt that "the missionaries should not speak openly on matters related to the disturbances lest it be used by the government to get missionaries sent out of the country."

"They stated that the missionaries should take a back seat in these matters and stand behind their Nigerian counterparts and let them do the speaking on these important matters," wrote Brown. "They stated that they would do anything that they could to protect the missionary but in the interest of our witness for Christ, we should not speak out on these things that had political implications."

Some in the meeting said that the government would listen to the Northern Christian Association, an organization led by Nigerians.

Bob Parham wrote to Cornell Goerner in Richmond, Virginia, on October 17, at the Southern Baptist Convention headquarters.

"I have been wanting to write but have hesitated to do so since the situation in Nigeria is difficult to interpret," he wrote.

He noted that missionaries were "not certain about the background of the well organized movement" that resulted in "mass killings of Ibos by northerners" and the desire to "eliminate Ibos."

Underscoring his intense work with the Jos airlift, Parham cryptically said, "All that has happened cannot be given in this letter."

Like her husband, Jo Ann Parham did not say much about what had happened. Nor did she know why little has been said publicly.

"I don't know why so little has been said about it [the genocide in Jos]. Maybe from a missionary standpoint not to stir up problems. Maybe to tone down between the races. And that could influence Christian witness there. Or people would be named and they would be in trouble…Maybe the world is not interested," said Parham.

One missionary who did seek to have a public discussion at Hillcrest was shut down, essentially reprimanded.

"I remember getting in a little difficulty with Paul Weaver, who was the principal of Hillcrest," said Lutheran teacher Beverly Knuth. "I was called into his office and questioned about an assignment that I had given to the students. It must have been an assignment for the older students, the seventh and eighth graders, because I had asked them to write an essay about what had happened in Jos. And how they felt about it."

She believed that "one of the house parents must have seen the exercise or read the student paper or something, because I think they went to the principal and said, 'What's this woman doing? Is this bad for the kids to be talking about or feeling or whatever?!'"

Knuth said, "I never was told who brought it to his attention. But I was told by him that I was not to do that, that it was not a good thing to do."

Although she disagreed with Weaver's instructions, she followed them. She thought it was a good exercise for the students. Nonetheless, she felt badly about having given the assignment.

"I guess I don't have an explanation for why we [the faculty] didn't talk about it. Or why we were maybe told not to. I can't remember being told to except in the relation to the assignment I asked the students to write. I don't know why we didn't," said Knuth. "If people were afraid, if we talked about it too much and we were too critical we would get in trouble with the government."

"We were living in their country. And they were in charge. And we were not. We were guests," she said. "It was our responsibility to kind of kowtow to what they wanted us to do. And we could get in trouble. And maybe that was our fear. And maybe that's why we kept our mouths shut…I don't know."

High school senior Ruth Keeney said, "We as high schoolers thought that if we didn't talk about it, it would go away. I'm wondering if the adults…responsible for all these young people…what's the best thing I can do to protect them, prevent them from seeing more of what they have already seen? And that's to normalize everything in their life as much as possible, which means not to get into deep conversations about what is going on."

"I do know that nobody knew for sure if we were safe," said Keeney, who lived at the Church of the Brethren Boulder Hill Hostel.

Carrie Robison, too, said the atrocities were not discussed widely or often.

The Assemblies of God high school student said, "It was very hard to talk about, because of the things we had seen and experienced were so far out of our normal life experience it was almost impossible to know what to do…We did talk about it. But I can't say that there were any big gatherings around a camp fire and we shared stories."

"Some of the kids didn't process it as well as others and some couldn't talk about it, wouldn't talk about it. And some just didn't know what to say," she said.

She didn't remember any formal discussions with teachers or school counselors.

Robison did talk to her parents, who lived in Aba in the Eastern Region.

When she returned to the United States, she shared with a few church youth groups, although the experiences were not understood.

"The fact that it has remained such an unexplored event in history has always baffled me," she said. "I couldn't understand why when I would talk about some things I would get a blank stare."

Sudan Interior Missionary MK John Price thought that missionaries and missionary children didn't talk publicly about the events because they didn't want to affiliate with any one side. Or they thought it wasn't "as big a deal on the world scale as it was."

"As an adult now, I think we just didn't process it…As a kid, you just absorb stuff. You lock it away. And years later, you realized how horrible it was," he said.

Price didn't recall "a single word" about it among the teachers.

"I was surprised by the emotions it brought up because I don't remember any emotional feelings at the time. What it made me realize is that we compartmentalize different things…It sits there," said Price. "I was transcribing my diary when it made me emotional. I couldn't stop the tears just reading it, typing it. I was on an airline flight. I felt drained."

"I suppose I talked about some of it," said Beverly Knuth, who served in Nigeria for 15 years. "I don't think I ever talked about what happened in Jos. It's not something you want people to know much about, especially if you're speaking to a women's group and you want support for your mission work… It might turn them off. So, I don't think I talked about it a lot."

She said one has a tendency to remember the good and not the bad.

Upon reviewing letters written to his family in the United States, Harvey Kiekover said he didn't say a whole lot about what he had witnessed in Makurdi. He did share contextually with church groups on furlough about what had happened, as well as the story about Linus and Oko.

He said he never felt like he was "being muzzled" by CRC leadership in Grand Rapids. He did feel that he should be cautious.

Phyllis Wagner said she doesn't remember talking about what happened among her fellow faculty members. "I didn't talk about it."

She did share a year later while on furlough in churches some of what had happened. "But I don't like over-sentimentalized stories…I didn't want any drama out of it…Yes, I told them about it then with the idea to pray for the country."

Bill and Audrey Cowley said that they didn't talk publicly about what they had witnessed and done at the Baptist High School.

"This is the first time we've talked about protecting the six Igbos at our school," said Audrey Cowley, who didn't recall ever talking in churches about the genocide in Nigeria.

She did say that the missionaries did talk among themselves about how terrible the events were and what they could do to prevent such future events.

"For many years after the experiences there, it was too painful to remember," said Bill Cowley. "I think immediately after and for the next few years, though, we didn't say anything because there were still political ramifications. We knew there were people who were close up to the situation in a political sense. And if we said too much about what we had done and questioned who did what, why, when and so forth. So, we thought it was just prudent not to say anything about it."

After they returned to the United States, "it was painful to remember," he said. "And you didn't like to speak so much about the sensational…People find it difficult to understand."

Audrey added, "The idea of human beings killing human beings right and left, it was something I couldn't bring myself to talk about. It was painful."

"I think there is another factor that came to play even in more recent years," said Bill Cowley. "There were people in churches here who really seriously questioned our wisdom" about hiding and smuggling people to the airport. They wondered "if we were being fair to our children, for example, to expose them to whatever danger there might have been. And so, we chose not to talk about it."

A half-century later, SUM missionary Dean Petersen contended, "I think the world needs to know what happened…It is very important to remember genocide."

Chapter 21

Rescue and Redemption

Having watched their faculty members and students depart, Bill and Audrey returned home—exhausted. The longest day of their lives was finally over. There would be little rest, however. The next day required the resumption of the daily schedule at the Baptist High School.

They were relieved that their colleagues and students were out of danger in the North. They did wonder how they were doing, what they were doing in the East.

"We didn't hear anything from any of them for months and months. We never could understand why we could not get any word from them. Whether they were afraid to try to contact us or whether there was just no means of contacting [with] things being in such shambles. So, we didn't hear for a long, long time," said Bill Cowley.

He did not know that after they had arrived in Lagos, they found a bus to take them to the East.

As for Jonathan Ikerionwu, he soon reached his family's home village of Okwelle, some 37 miles from Oweri. He found, to his surprise, his mother. He had not known in Jos that shortly after his brother had spoken to Cowley, his mother and younger siblings had decided to leave the North for the Eastern Region rather than face an uncertain future. She was surprised and happy to see him. She asked how he escaped—he told her the story.

The years dragged by without a word from those who had been flown to safety, albeit short-lived safety when the civil war erupted in 1967.

The Igbos had declared their independence with the establishment of the Republic of Biafra. The Igbos sought to separate from Nigeria—Nigeria was determined to suppress the rebellion. If one tribe could secede, then other tribes might follow suit, splintering apart the "giant of Africa." Neither the federal government nor the British government wanted that to happen.

Over the course of three years, an estimated 1.5 million Biafrans died from starvation. Church groups and the International Red Cross flew in food and medical supplies at night, mostly at risk. The Nigerian government charged that the relief-supply flights were really a cover for shipping weapons into the country. Sensitive to that accusation, Christian leaders diligently checked arriving flights to make sure arms were not being smuggled abroad.

The TV images of skeletal children shook the American public. They demanded the intervention of the United States government. President Lyndon Johnson felt so much public pressure at one point that he reportedly told the State Department, "Just get those [expletive] babies off my TV set," according to *The New Yorker*.

Even with his authorization for relief aid, it wasn't enough. Despite their best intentions and efforts, humanitarians could not ship in enough relief supplies to ward off the deepening malnutrition and disease.

Their supply efforts were also hamstrung by the Nigerian air force's bombing of the Uli airstrip, where supplies were flown in.

During the civil war, Ikerionwu remained in his village "doing absolutely nothing," he said. All schools in the East were closed, including the Baptist High School in Port Harcourt. So, pursuing his education was out of the question.

"Luckily, I was not conscripted. One time they came to conscript me into the Biafran Army, my mother raised all kinds of alarm. People told them what happened to me and they just let me go," he said.

Ikerionwu did not know what had happened to his father and the eldest brother in Bukuru. The family lived for three years without news from or about them.

"We were not exactly sure what happened especially during the civil war," he said. When the few people—who had remained in hiding—began to return after the civil war, his father and brother did not. Several weeks later, they concluded, "they did not survive."

As the dust settled after the war, he received a letter from the Cowleys encouraging him to return to school. The Cowleys did not receive a response from Ikerionwu, no doubt leaving them with questions about his survival.

Ikerionwu faced an impasse. As the eldest male in the family, he was expected to provide for the family. But he had no job and no prospects of a job. The family was the poorest family in his village. He had the responsibility to care for them. He thought employment opportunities might exist in Jos. His mother opposed his return to the North. After some discussion, he prayed God would give him guidance. He decided to go back to Jos—to the Baptist High School.

Surviving the genocide in 1966 and the three-year civil war was a miracle of sorts for Igbos from northern Nigeria. To return safely to the North and to find employment would require another miracle.

One such miracle occurred in Jos one bright morning.

"I was in the chapel at the school. It was early in the morning. We were having our regular morning chapel time. When you are up at the pulpit facing the back of the chapel, where the main door is for the chapel…there was a huge window there and the sunlight was so bright in that window. So, if someone came in the door, you only saw a silhouette, you really couldn't tell who it was," said Cowley.

"Well, the door opened and someone came in. Naturally, you would think maybe it was a student running late or a teacher running late and they were just slipping in quietly."

That was not the case, however.

"This individual continued to walk on down the aisle slowly, and I would say pretty unsteadily, till he got to the front. He was almost unrecognizable. He was so emaciated, so dirty, so disheveled," he said. "But we could make out that this was indeed Jonathan."

Ikerionwu had returned to school. He had left without finishing his course work. He wanted to finish it. "He was coming back to take his place," said Cowley.

"When Bill came from school and told me that Jonathan had come to the chapel that morning, I was thrilled," said Audrey Cowley. "But he said that Jonathan was very thin, very sickly. So, of course, I put something together to help him build up his strength. He went to classes, but we also gave him nourishment. And helped him get back to his normal self."

By looking at him, she knew that he had suffered a lot, as she had heard that "Biafra suffered."

"It was a thing of joy...It was a fantastic reunion," Ikerionwu recalled. "The Cowleys...employed me to be the house master. I worked in the library. I acted as a labor master. I was doing all kinds of things in the school. They paid me for it."

He applied to Ahmadu Bello University in Zaria. Admission was not granted. He waited until the next year for admission without hearing a word of acceptance.

Meanwhile, Cowley had explored other options. He gave an application to Ikerionwu to attend Hesston College in Kansas, where he was accepted and given financial aid to attend.

Ikerionwu faced two more hurdles—transportation to the United States and care for his mother. To his great surprise, the Cowleys and others paid for his airplane ticket and gave him a 1,000 pounds to support his mother.

"This act...is one that has completely transformed the family to the extent today that...we are one of the most educated families in Okwelle now," not the poorest, he said.

Ikerionwu went on to earn a Ph.D. and obtain a teaching position at the University of Abuja, located in Nigeria's capital. He became a professor and deputy dean of faculty education.

"I owe my life...I'm alive today because of the Cowleys," he said tearfully.

Without the Cowleys, "I would definitely have died or would have been killed in 1966. I will ever remain grateful for them. I will never forget this single act of miraculous deed."

"It is a miracle that I escaped the pogrom," he said. "And not only that, that I even got an education is equally an act that I will never forget them for."

Chapter 22

Role of Missionaries in a Time of Genocide

Reflecting on the events of 50 years ago, missionaries readily acknowledged that they were unprepared to face what unfolded. They thought they did the best they could, given the restraints of being outsiders. Missionary children drew the same conclusions about their parents.

"If the government itself was unprepared to handle this kind of crisis, I don't see how a missionary could have been prepared," stated MK Carrie Robison. "The missionaries were reacting to the events that were happening right then."

"You fly by the seat of your pants or the grace of God in times like this. You have no training, no experience," said Harvey Kiekover. "We had no resources except to pray for godly wisdom and help us to do the right thing and not do more harm and more damage."

He said that he didn't know what to do about his Igbo employee, Oko, when the killings started in Makurdi. He felt obligated to save his life without knowing how. He feared that if he took Oko in his car to the train station that the mob might spot him and stop the car. They might drag Oko out of the car and kill him.

"You sense in a very real way that you are aliens in a foreign land. And you respect your status as a foreigner. This is not your country," he said, underscoring the restraints on what missionaries could do.

Dean Petersen, too, noted the limitations of engagement.

"I believe the missionaries did what they could," he said. "They did what they could to keep from getting too involved. We had to be careful. We could not choose sides…If people came by and they needed food, they were given food and then they went to places where they could hide."

Bill Cowley offered a similar observation. Missionaries had to avoid taking sides. They had to address immediate human needs.

"The role of a missionary in the time of genocide is to minister to human need. It is not really to take the side of one or the other against their enemies. That's not our role at that time. We might have at some time prior to that or sometime after that used that as an example to try to help people learn lessons of living with one another and how to treat one another," said Cowley. "It's your place to step up and minister to the needs that presented themselves."

The missionary's role was not to preach or teach or sort out people based on whether they were Christian or Muslim or pagan, Easterner or Northerner, stated Cowley. "We were responding as humanitarians…without any prejudice."

His wife, Audrey, said, "When the genocide started in Jos, we just tried to follow what we thought the Lord was leading us to do and that was to be responsible for those for whom we were responsible. To protect them and do whatever we could to keep them from being victims of genocide."

"Our role as missionaries was to comfort, to protect, to encourage, to do whatever we could do to help those in need," she said.

Meeting physical needs was the priority, contended Beverly Knuth.

The missionary task was to "offer assistance as much as possible in any way possible whether it's preparing food or if it's taking care of the wounded or if it is ministering in some other way. I think it has to be at least initially a physical involvement…It's not just, 'I'll pray for you.' I don't think that works…for people in a disaster situation. I think you have to be physically involved," she said.

Robison thought that for missionaries to be effective in times of crisis that they needed a long-term relationship with the people. "Missionaries can't just put on a superhero cape and fly into a crisis, work some magic and then fly out again to the next crisis."

"I watched missionaries do in this time of genocide what they were called to do…I would have been shocked if the missionaries hadn't done anything, because I was accustomed to seeing them in action," said Robison.

The missionary role was "to stand forward and help the oppressed and if necessary even to sacrifice their own life for their faith trying to save their fellow man," suggested Buzz Bowers.

Kiekover rejected the idea that the missionaries had to offer the same response to the crisis. "I don't think you can have a general policy on what you should do with genocide. Every context is going to be different."

For example, he said, what happened in Bukuru at the Theological College of Northern Nigeria could not have happened in Makurdi.

Interviewed missionaries and missionary children agreed that missionaries could not have stopped the atrocities. They were unaware of when it would start in late September. They didn't know which rumors to believe and which to ignore. They never could figure out who was behind the planning and directing the mobs.

"I don't think the missionaries could have done more to stop the atrocities," said MK Ruth Keeney.

In the midst of the crisis, Roger Ingold wrote Henry Long confessing some shortcomings in the missionary effort: "We regret that we have been so lax on some of our teaching related to reconciliation, individual and collective responsibility for social conditions…teaching on peace and non-violence and living together as brothers."

His confession was accompanied by an itemized list of the positive things the missionaries had done, mentioning Paul Weaver in particular. He was "under great pressure and strain" and he saved a life, perhaps referring to Hycenth Adibenma.

Recalling the close cooperation among the different denominations, Ingold said, "Nearly all of us were involved in one way or another in getting medical attention, food, refuge, transportation…At one time a missionary operated the airport tower and radio so that planes could get in and out. Missionaries operated switchboards and kept alive some communications which were essential."

Missionary kids, or MKs, also drew his praise. He mentioned his older son, John, who had gone to the police station to help out. Ingold shared that he didn't know what his son had done until later on.

Ingold wrote that the MKs "demanded that they be allowed to join in on the relief operation. They did so with real courage."

Writing to Long on October 15, Chalmer Faw bragged on the MK involvement: "Hillcrest students protected, aided, ministered to and fed victims of violence, often at the risk of their own lives."

Hillcrest teacher Carl Eisman saw high school students doing what they could at the police station. "They were bandaging wounds. They were cooking stew…They were sitting and praying with people. These were kids. It was amazing."

Serving was part of their DNA, he said. "They rose to the occasion."

Ingold told Long: "We had a great number of heroes."

Timeline of Events

1960

Sat., Oct. 1 — Nigeria celebrates independence from Britain

1966

Sat., Jan. 15 — Military coup; Nigeria's leaders are assassinated

Sun., Jan. 16 — Major-General Johnson Aguiyi-Ironsi, an Igbo, emerges in power

Tue., May 24 — Ironsi issues the "unification decree," which Northern Region leaders see as an attempt to curtail their power

Sat., May 28 — Several days of demonstrations begin in the Northern Region; Igbos killed en masse

Fri., July 29 — Counter-coup; Ironsi kidnapped and later found dead

Mon., Aug. 1 — Lt.-Col. Yakubu Gowon, a Christian from a minority tribe in the North, emerges in power

Wed., Sep. 21 — A genocide against Igbos begins in parts of the Northern Region

Wed., Sep. 28 — The genocide strikes Jos, home to a large missionary community

Fri., Sept. 30 — Wounded Igbos and Easterners begin fleeing to the Jos police compound for refuge

Sat., Oct. 1 — Missionaries, missionary kids and others begin organizing aid to the wounded at the Jos police compound

Sun., Oct. 2 — Evacuations of Igbos and Easterners back to the Eastern Region begin in Jos and continue for several days

Fri., Oct. 7 — Missionaries and Nigerian pastors hold a private, two-day meeting in Jos to discuss "the disturbances"

1967

Fri., May 26 — Eastern Region votes to secede from Nigeria

Tue., May 30 — Biafra created

Thu., July 6 — Nigeria begins military action against Biafra

1970

Thu., Jan. 15 — Civil war ends and Biafra reintegrated into Nigeria

Glossary of Terms

Coup d'état: A French term that refers to the overthrow of a government, usually by force.

Emir: Derived from the Arabic word for "commander" or "prince," it is a common title for a Muslim ruler or leader (chief) in a nation or region.

Igbo and Ibo: Igbo is the name of the tribe whose homeland was the Eastern Region of Nigeria. Igbo is the contemporary spelling. The tribal name was often spelled Ibo in correspondence of missionaries.

Mallam: A Muslim religious teacher. It is a title of honor given to Muslim educators.

Nigeria: Located in western Africa along the Gulf of Guinea, the nation borders Benin (west), Niger (north), Chad (northeast) and Cameroon (east).

Premier: The head of government in a nation or region.

Tribal markings: A longtime practice in Nigeria used as a means of identifying a person as a member of a particular family or tribe in which a cut is made in a particular pattern or location on newborns that form scars.

www.ingramcontent.com/pod-product-compliance
Lightning Source LLC
Chambersburg PA
CBHW062221080426
42734CB00010B/1981